/

...And Oft

In his engaging new book, Rabbi Stephen Fuchs takes us on a journey of healing and hope to Germany then and now. The personal narratives and painful remembrances are framed with uplifting teachings that testify to the resilience of the human spirit.

Rabbi Rick Jacobs, President, Union for Reform Judaism

Rabbi Stephen Fuchs helps the reader travel through places and time to understand the Jewish people's history in Europe. His insights – which are on the mark – reveal the deep humanity and hope that characterize his own life and actions.

Stéphane Beder, Senior Vice Chair,
World Union for Progressive Judaism, Paris, France

It takes bravery, compassion and fortitude to teach and remind the world about one of the darkest stains of humanity – the Holocaust. Rabbi Stephen Fuchs does this with an unwavering zeal for sharing the truth and inspiring peace and interfaith dialogue through his mission work in Germany.

Ella Nayor, Florida Weekly award winning journalist, author,
speaker, and community outreach educator for human rights;
Fort Lauderdale, Florida

We need to know Jews, all of us. With anti-Semitism rising sharply again across Europe, I am grateful that so many Germans are able to encounter Rabbi Stephen and Vickie Fuchs – rebutting prejudice and building bridges.

Claudia Linker Monnet, Principal
ALS Aktivierende LernSysteme, Flensburg, Germany

A wonderful collection of stories full of optimism: Rabbi Fuchs and his wife, Vickie, encounter the Nazi past and meet, wherever they go, people of all ages ready to confront this difficult legacy and heal the wounds of history and to make the world "a more just, caring and compassionate place" – a phrase that likely remains in the memories of everyone who hears Rabbi Fuchs speak.

Walter Joshua Pannbacker, Ritual Leader,
Reform Jewish Community of Kiel, Germany

Stephen Fuchs, Rabbi and educator, recounts his presence at the historic churches and synagogues of Germany, especially in Leipzig, Friedrichstadt, Kaltenkirchen, Husum, Kiel, and Edinburgh, Scotland, to establish an important connection with the past. He reflects on the horrors of Kristallnacht and recounts the arrest of his father, Leo Fuchs, on that night. The book is a heartrending tribute by a loving son to his father that reflects on this tragic time in history and forges a path forward toward a more hopeful future.

Sally Wolff-King, PhD, Woodruff Health Sciences Historian,
Emory University, Atlanta, Georgia

...And Often the First Jew

by

Rabbi Stephen Lewis Fuchs

For Christine —
With best wishes
for good health!
Steve

I've enjoyed
meeting you. Here's
to good health!
Vickie

Mazo Publishers

And Often the First Jew

ISBN 978-1-946124-54-8

Contact The Author
www.rabbifuchs.com
Follow Rabbi Fuchs
on Twitter: @rabbifuchs6
and on Facebook

Mazo Publishers
Chaim Mazo, Publisher
P.O. Box 36084 ~ Jerusalem 91360 Israel
P.O. Box 10474 ~ Jacksonville, FL 32247 USA

Website: www.mazopublishers.com
Bookstore: www.mazopub.com
Email: mazopublishers@gmail.com

54321

For our partners in Germany,
Ursula Sieg, Martin Pommerening, and Wolfgang Henke.

To my wonderful mother-in-law, Stefanie Steinberg,
for the many ways she inspires me ...

And for Vickie,
who makes it all worthwhile!

Table of Contents

Acknowledgments 8
Foreword by Rabbi Walter Homolka 10
Preface 12

Chapter 1
Toward Mutual Respect and Understanding

A Trip I Had to Make 16
Why I am Going to Germany 21
En Route 25
As I Travel to Germany: Elul Thoughts (III) 26
A Most Meaningful Way to Mark Kristallnacht 28
Bishop Mussinghoff:
An Extraordinary Friend of the Jews 30
The Church of the Broken Cross 32
Discussing Psalms at the U. of Hamburg 34
An Unforgettable 10 Weeks in Germany 36
So, Rabbi, What do You *Really* Think About Jesus? 39
How a 94-year-old Jewish Woman's Friendship
with German Students Changed Them All 41

Chapter 2
Anti-Semitism

O, The Chimney! 44
My First Swastika 46
A Long-Deferred Visit: Auschwitz 48
At Dachau 51
A Purim Message from Bad Segeberg in 1936 53
Learning from the Past; Facing the Future 56
Paris: Hope in the Face of Terror 59
Back to Kaltenkirchen 62
To Welcome the Stranger 64

Chapter 3
Leipzig

Letter to my Father...Leipzig Zoo 68
Why I Have Come to Leipzig 71
Thomaskirche Kristallnacht Speech 73
Was it a Miracle? 78
Return to the Leipzig Zoo 83

Chapter 4
Vickie's Perspective

Confronting My Fear of Kraków 86
A Weekend of Opposites, or Was It? 89
A Newfound Compassion 94
From Breslau to Neumünster:
A Long Journey Home 98

Chapter 5
Kiel

Rita and Horst 104
Return to Friedrichstadt 106
A Ray of Light that Pierced the Darkness 108

Chapter 6
Pastors' Conventions

Why We Should Thank Eve for
Our Lives of Meaning 112
Pastors' Convention in Breklum 115

Chapter 7
Family and Friends

Yahrzeit in Edinburgh 118
The Parsonage Has a Sukkah! 121
Haedicke 124
Ulrike 126
The Lehrer 129
Rita Goldberg 131

Acknowledgments

I am most grateful to the Union for Reform Judaism and the editors of its website blog, Ms. Jane Herman and Ms. Kate Kaput for permission to republish several of the essays in this book which I originally wrote for ReformJudaism.org.

I am grateful to Mr. Chaim Mazo of Mazo Publishers for the confidence he has shown in this book.

Profound thanks also to Professor Walter Homolka for the many ways in which he has rekindled the flame of non-Orthodox Jewish life in Europe and for the very gracious Foreword he has written for this volume.

I owe a deep debt of gratitude to Walter Joshua Pannbacker, Hartmut Bomhoff, Dvora Themal, Pastorin Anke Wolff-Steger, Pfarrerin Britta Taddiken, Pastor Timoteus Arndt, Alexandra Wilczura, Jan Kirschenbaum, Pfarrerin Simone Berger-Lober, Rabbi Zsolt Balla, Bishop Heinrich Mussinghoff, Dr. Claudia Linker, Rita and Horst Blunk, Dr. Keren-Miriam Först Haedicke, Imam Halima Krausen, Pastorin Ulrike Wohlfahrt, Pastorin Martina Dittkrist, Probst Daniel Havemann, Probst Stefan Block, Pastor Friedmann Madegaard, Dr. Cornelia, Krüger, Sylvia Schriebe, Dr. Navah Kaddish, Walter Blender, Dr. Klaus Rittman, and Pastorin Stefanie Kämpf, for all they have done to facilitate our work in Germany.

Susan Shuman has been my agent, coach, web designer, advocate and friend since we worked together on *What's in It for Me? Finding Ourselves in Biblical Narratives* in 2014. Without her guidance and skill, this book would never have seen the light of day.

Vickie's mother, Stefanie Steinberg, has been the inspiration for our work. Her Life's Journey inspires all that we do in Germany. As well, Pastorin Ursula Sieg, her husband Pastor Martin Pommerening along with Wolfgang Henke from the Holstenschule in Neumünster arranged the exhibit about Vickie's mother that has been the basis of all the teaching we have done in German schools. It is to the four of them that I dedicate this book along with ...

אחרון אחרון חביב – Lastly and most important: Vickie has shared every step of our experience in Germany and for forty-five years of marriage to me. Words cannot express the depth of my debt to and love for her, and I pray we share many more years together.

Stephen Lewis Fuchs
Sanibel, Florida
Purim 5779

Foreword

by
Rabbi Walter Homolka PhD PhD DHL

In 2011, Rabbi Stephen Fuchs made his first trip to Germany. At the time, he was President of the World Union for Progressive Judaism. In September 2011 he initiated a program of study about, and reconciliation with, post-war Germany. Eight years later, the program is still in place.

At the time he met with leading political figures such as the foreign secretary, the ministers of the interior and of, and also honored the resistance fighters of July 20, 1944 around Claus Schenk Graf von Stauffenberg at the German Resistance Memorial Center together with Germany's defense secretary.

In his capacity as president of the WUPJ, Rabbi Fuchs traveled to over 65 communities on six continents fostering Reform Jewish values and legitimacy. But to Rabbi Stephen Fuchs, Germany was set apart. The Holocaust is a driving force in his life. The Rabbi's late father, Leo Fuchs, was arrested in Leipzig, Germany on Kristallnacht, November 9, 1938, abused, and sent to the Dachau Prison Camp where my grandfather had also been incarcerated. Fortunately, there were relatives in the United States who secured Leo Fuchs' release after a short time, and he came to the U.S.A.

So, Stephen Lewis Fuchs has a special bond with Germany as does and his wife Victoria Steinberg Fuchs. Her mother was born in Breslau and her father grew up in Essen. Stephen and Vickie's relationship grew stronger and deeper during the time they'd spent in Germany, thanks to Pastorin Ursula Sieg and her husband Pastor Martin Pommerening.

In 2014, Rabbi Fuchs accepted the gracious invitation of Pastorin Martina Dittkrist and became the first rabbi ever to give a sermon in the Michaelis-Kirche in Kaltenkirchen. Rabbi Fuchs' sermon was received as a gesture of forgiveness to the church and acknowledgment of its atonement for the fact that the one-time Pastor, Ernst Biberstein, who left the church to become a Nazi officer, was found guilty at Nuremburg for atrocities committed against thousands of Jews, and their subsequent deaths.

On November 6, 2015, Rabbi Fuchs conducted the first Jewish service in the city of Friedrichstadt, Germany, since Kristallnacht and accepted an invitation from the then bishop of Aachen, Heinrich Mussinghoff, to deliver a lecture on the occasion of the fiftieth anniversary of the Nostra Aetate at which the Catholic Church officially absolved Jews of responsibility for Jesus' death – a milestone for Catholic-Jewish relations.

Over the last four years, Rabbi Fuchs and his wife Vickie have met many Germans – Jewish and non-Jewish. This book is a fascinating account of these encounters. I am grateful for this transatlantic bridge that Stephen and Vickie have built since 2011.

Rabbi Walter Homolka PhD PhD DHL
Rector, Abraham Geiger College, Berlin
Chairman, Union of Progressive Jews in Germany

Preface

It is a heady but eerie feeling to preach in a church with a cornerstone with the year 1220 on it and to have one of the community leaders inform you that you are the first rabbi to preach there in the church's history. "Many of our worshipers," he continued, "have never seen a Jew before."

It was not a unique example. When I spoke in German churches in towns and villages like Schulensee, Kaltenkirchen, Bordesholm, Husum, Friedrichstadt and even in cities as large as Leipzig, Neumünster or Kiel, I was almost always the first rabbi to ever speak there, and for many worshipers, I was the first living Jew that the worshipers had ever seen.

To be "the first" is both a privilege and a burden. I am ever-mindful the impression those to whom I speak will have of Jews and Judaism depends on what I say and the way I say it.

For four years it has been my privilege and that of my wife Vickie to spend part of the year in Germany. There, in addition to my work in synagogues and churches, we teach together in German high schools about the Holocaust. To facilitate our lessons, we use a wonderful exhibit about Vickie's own 97-year-old mother, Stefanie Steinberg. She was born in Breslau and was uprooted along with her family in 1936 when the Nazi government informed her father, a respected Radiologist who had served in the German army during World War I that he could no longer be a physician in Germany. The family moved to Barcelona, but after the Civil War erupted in Spain, the family dispersed, and Stefanie lived in a Kinderheim in Switzerland. When she was 17, she made her way to New York and eventually to Los Angeles and San Francisco.

High School students find her story enthralling, and some have reached out to connect with her personally. Almost all the students to whom we speak have never seen a rabbi before; many have never seen a Jew.

"Being the first" causes Vickie and I to feel a special responsibility similar to the one I feel when I speak or teach in German churches. We want students to know about the Shoah, and its horrors. But I constantly say to students and parishioners to whom I speak:

Wir können die Vergangenheit nicht ungeschehen machen, aber wir können gemeinsam an einer besseren Zukunft arbeiten.

We cannot undo the past,
but the future is ours to shape.

If in some small way, our experiences in Germany and the essays in this book can somehow contribute to that *besseren Zukunft* – that better future, our efforts will be amply rewarded.

Rabbi Stephen Lewis Fuchs
Sanibel, Florida
Purim 5779

Chapter 1

Toward Mutual Respect and Understanding

A Trip I Had to Make

Fall, 1968

I first found out what happened on this night in 1938 when I began my graduate studies to become a rabbi at the Hebrew Union College in Los Angeles. At the opening convocation the then dean and later President of the College, Rabbi Alfred Gottschalk, of blessed memory, told of how as an eight-year-old child in the town of Oberwesel, he watched his grandfather wade into the river Rhine to save charred scraps of Torah scrolls thrown by the Nazis from his burning synagogue.

Summer, 1982

As my train pulled into Leipzig's huge station, I realized that my first glimpse of the city was probably my father's last as he traveled on a different kind of train to Dachau after his arrest on Kristallnacht, November 9, 1938.

I picked up a detailed city map at the information center to try to find the street and apartment where my father had grown up. I also sought the location of the city zoo.

The Zoo

Why the zoo? The eyewitness report on Kristallnacht by David H. Buffum, American consul in Leipzig, reveals: "Jewish dwellings were smashed into, and the contents looted ... An eighteen-year-old boy was hurled from a three-story window to land with both legs broken ... Three synagogues were fired simultaneously by incendiary bombs, and many Jews were rounded up and thrown into the stream that flows through the city zoo. SS men commanded horrified spectators to spit, jeer, and defile them with mud."

When I arrived at the entrance to the zoo, it was 6:45

p.m. The gatekeeper said I was too late. "The zoo closes at seven."

"It is all right," I answered, as I handed over the entrance fee. "I only need to go in for a few minutes." The gatekeeper protested, but I persisted until she finally let me pass.

In a few minutes I was standing before the stream. Tears came to my eyes as I heard myself asking out loud, "Is this where they took you, Papa? Did those bastards spit on you...? Did they throw mud on you?" Then, as if in retaliation, I spit into the water from a bridge that straddles the stream.

67 Jews in Leipzig *

The next morning, I found the office of the Leipzig Jewish community. The elderly lady who answered the door explained that the head of the community was out but would be back later. I explained to her that my father grew up in Leipzig. She pulled down a dusty ledger and opened it to the F's. I quickly found the family listing.

While we were talking, the leader of the community walked in. I explained who I was and why I was there. He was warm, friendly, and clearly pleased that I had come.

I asked him, "How many Jews live in Leipzig?"

"67," he answered.

"And how many lived here," I continued, "when the Jewish population was at its peak?"

"In 1935," he responded, "18,000 Jews lived in Leipzig."

"How many perished during the Holocaust?" I asked.

"14,000," he replied.

The twelve-hour train ride to Amsterdam gave me plenty of time to digest my experiences in Leipzig. I thought, of course, of my father. After Kristallnacht, the Nazis took him to Dachau where they shaved his head, interrogated him, and abused him.

---

* Today, because of immigration from the Former Soviet Union, some 1,300 Jews live in Leipzig.

But Leo Fuchs was one of the lucky ones. Because he had relatives already in the United States, and because his visas were complete and in order, the American consulate secured his release after only a few days.

He never spoke of any of this to me, but I know the trauma's effect never left him. In the spring of 1969 my father fell gravely ill. I flew home to New Jersey from my rabbinical studies in Los Angeles to be with him. I shall never forget my feelings of helplessness when I entered the hospital room, and my father in a semi-comatose state did not recognize me.

I stood there and shuddered as he began shouting in German – which he never spoke at home – that the guards should stop beating him! He had repressed those memories for more than 30 years.

And they were – by and large – good years! In this country my father found love and raised a family. But I – perhaps irrationally – blame the Nazis for shortening his life and depriving me of sharing my greatest joys with him: My ordination as a rabbi, my marriage to Vickie, and our children and our grandchildren.

Our children! They are our people's answer to Hitler's madness. For us Jews each new life represents a young sapling planted not only to bring joy to a family but also to revitalize a once verdant forest ravaged by fire, by smoke, and by gas.

The word, "Genocide," which we throw around so loosely today, came into our vocabulary so that we could attempt to define what Hitler tried to do: to extirpate the gene pool of our people.

And so we command ourselves: זכור (*Zachor*) Remember! But if we only remember to wallow in our sorrow, then we waste our time and our tears. We must remember what was so that we can make what will be better.

How could God allow the Holocaust?

People ask me all the time, "How could God allow the Holocaust?" I answer that God gave human beings free will and placed us in charge of and responsible for this world. Without free will life would have no meaning. We human beings would be mere puppets on a string or actors following a script from which we could not deviate.

God yearns for us to create a world of justice and compassion, but God does not do it for us. When we fail, it is our failure, not God's. When we fail, I believe God weeps with us and for us.

A Miraculous Vision

As I walked away from the stream that flows through the Leipzig zoo, I wandered past a den of timber wolves in a natural enclosure and beheld a truly wondrous site. A mother wolf stood stark still, with two suckling pups nursing blissfully.

At first, I thought it so incongruous to see such an exquisite glimpse of nature's harmony in a place that represented to me only discord and destruction. Yet, that is the image that lingered in my mind during the long train ride back to Amsterdam. My mind's eye kept returning from the vision of violence, hatred, and pain to the peaceful, pastoral scene of wolf pups drawing sustenance and strength from their mother.

The Leipzig zoo will always represent for me the horrible evil of which humanity is capable. The wolves, though, will always represent harmony God wants us to create in this world.

On Yom Kippur we read in our synagogue one of the Torah's most important texts: "See I have set before you life and goodness, death and evil" (Dt. 30:15). The choice is ours, but God exhorts us: "Choose life that you and your offspring may live" (Dt. 30:19).

No, the question is not where God was during the Holocaust. The question is, "Where was humanity?"

We cannot change the past, but the future is ours to shape.

We know too well that we can choose death, but God hopes our past will strengthen us as we face the future.

Yes, we can choose death, but God hopes:

That the pain we relive this night will give us the courage

To clothe the naked,

Feed the hungry,

Teach the unlettered,

Foster understanding among all people,

And use the vast talents – with which God has blessed us –

To choose life, and

To forge a world of justice, caring, compassion and peace!

Why I am Going to Germany

In a recent meeting the head of Germany's United Jewish Appeal, Nathan Norman Gelbart, said in his address that the German Jewish community is scared "because these are things that have not occurred since 1933."

Random attacks on Jews and Jewish groups in Europe testify that anti-Semitism is on the rise again in Europe as my wife Vickie and I prepare to embark September 14 on a ten-week stay in Germany to work in synagogues, schools, and Lutheran churches to promote greater understanding and mutual respect.

The emotional highlight of the visit will doubtless come on November 9 when I speak at the annual Kristallnacht - known in Germany as Pogromnacht - commemoration at the famed Thomaskirche in Leipzig, the magnificent church where Martin Luther once preached and where Johann Sebastian Bach served as organist and choirmaster from 1723 until he died in 1750.

My father Leo Fuchs was arrested on Kristallnacht, an event that has both haunted and inspired me since I first learned about it in 1969. When my son, Leo Fuchs - a school principal named for my father - heard that I would speak there, he immediately made arrangements to fly to Leipzig from his home in San Francisco for the occasion. My cousin Irene is also coming from London.

This will be my third visit to the city where my father was born, grew up and where (as three sterling dishes that I treasure attest) he won citywide doubles championships in table tennis in 1929, 30 and 33, the year Hitler came to power.

My first two visits could not have been more different. In 1982, I was turned away at the East German border crossing, Oebisfelde, when I naively told the passport inspector that I was a rabbi on my way to Leipzig to visit the city of my father's youth. Only after a day-long detour to Berlin where I reinvented myself as an art teacher eager to visit Leipzig's famous museums did I receive a visa.

At that time the Jewish communal headquarters in Leipzig was a tiny dusty, hard to find cramped suite of offices that I reached by climbing a creaky, narrow staircase. The head of the community informed me at the time 67 Jews lived in Leipzig. In 1935, there were 18,000, 14,000 of whom perished in the Shoah.

When Vickie and I visited in 2011, by contrast, we found the spacious Jewish community offices in a lovely refurbished synagogue. The young rabbi of Leipzig's Jewish community – revitalized by the arrival of hundreds of Russian immigrants – personally guided us to the places where my relatives lived.

Ursula Sieg, regional Pastor for Church-School Relations of the Evangelical-Lutheran Church of North Germany, is painstakingly coordinating our upcoming pilgrimage with a packed schedule of sermons, lectures and dialogues. Her motivation is to have Germans learn about Judaism and further Germany's yeoman efforts to promote mutual understanding and respect. She has enlisted and received moral and financial support from the Förderverein Judentum in Schleswig-Holstein (Society for Support of Judaism in Schleswig-Holstein), the Progressive Jewish Community of Kiel and the Abraham Geiger College in Berlin and Potsdam for these efforts. We are very grateful to Pastor Sieg and all of those who are contributing to making our visit a reality.

Last winter when Pastor Sieg first proposed the idea to me, it seemed a natural step in the remarkable progress Germany has made to atone for the horrors of the Hitler era. For example, in 2011 and 2012 as president of the

World Union for Progressive Judaism, I signed papers that helped lead to the establishment of the School of Jewish Theology at the University of Potsdam. The agreements paved the way for the formal arrangements for the German government to fully fund the new institute, which offers B.A. and M.A. programs to students from Germany and beyond, including those studying to be rabbis and cantors. I look forward eagerly to returning to Potsdam to lecture and interact with students and faculty at the school.

With recent developments, though, the entire timbre of my visit has changed. Now my joyful anticipation is tempered by the reality that anti-Semitism in Europe – and even in Germany where anti-Jewish demonstrations are barred by law – is surfacing once again.

"Why are you going there," people have asked? "You will do as much good as one bailing water from a rising river with a teaspoon." Their challenge makes me toss and turn at night. I certainly do not believe I can cure the world, Europe or specific Germans of anti-Semitism. But I am also heartened by the way the German government – beginning with Chancellor Angela Merkel – and most of the German people officially and forcefully condemn anti-Semitism.

Still I am wary. The current war in Israel and Gaza – and the world's reaction to Israel's efforts to protect its citizens from the terror of Hamas whose very existence is predicated on Israel's destruction – gives credence once again to the notion that we Jews are, as the Moabite seer Balaam proclaimed long ago, "a people that dwells alone" (Numbers 23:9).

But still I will go. I will go with joy and gratitude for the people that invited me. I will go with the knowledge that many in Germany are eager to learn about the faith and way of life that gave birth to Christianity.

On my first visit to Leipzig, I had to visit the city zoo because on Kristallnacht the Jews of the city were rounded up and made to stand in the stream that flows through it. There, former neighbors and friends spat on them, jeered them and threw mud on them. In 1982 I stood on a bridge that straddles that stream weeping inside as I imagined my father standing in the water on that horrible night in 1938.

But as I was leaving the zoo, I walked past a den of timber wolves where a cub was nursing in peaceful bliss at his mother's breast. That scene etched itself into my heart as a symbol of the harmony that God wants us to strive for in this world.

I don't expect anti-Semitism to disappear because I will spend ten weeks in Germany, but I feel that destiny is calling me to do my best. If enough people pick up their teaspoons and join the effort, we can stop the rising waters of anti-Semitism from overflowing.

En Route

For the third year Vickie and I are *en route* to Germany to lead worship for the Days of Awe, to teach two seminars at Geiger College, to teach high school students about the Shoah, and to speak in churches and synagogues. It is a great privilege for us to do our tiny part to help replant Jewish life where Hitler ravaged it with smoke, fire and gas.

And yet –

Some say, "You are wasting your time! Do you really think you make a difference?"

I cannot be sure, but I believe it is the effort that counts. We all have a choice. We can use whatever talents we have to make the world a bit more caring and compassionate, or we can throw up our hands in despair and say, "It doesn't do any good, so why bother?"

The scoffers remind me of a story I first heard nearly 40 years ago when Rabbi David Saperstein told it to my congregation in Columbia, Maryland toward the end of his sermon.

Once a man went every day to the wicked city of Sodom urging the people to repent. His friends mocked him and called him a fool. "Don't you know," they sneered, "that those wicked people will never change and become like you?"

"Perhaps," the man allowed, "they will not change and become like me. But I will continue to bring them my message so that, God forbid, I do not change and become like them."

And so, we set out for Germany with hope and with joy. We know we cannot undo the past, but the future is ours to shape, and I am convinced that the German people want it to be better than the past. We cannot know if we shall make a difference, but we shall do our best and pray that God will bless our efforts.

As I Travel to Germany: Elul Thoughts (III)

One of my most precious possessions is a copy of the Talmudic tractate *Kiddushin* printed in Munich in 1946 on presses once used for Nazi propaganda. A Talmud printed on an erstwhile Nazi printing press is a powerful symbol of our privilege to use our time, our talent and our material resources to help replant vibrant, progressive Jewish learning and living in the places where the Nazis tried to destroy them.

In this volume (page 40B) we find one of the most uplifting of rabbinic teachings whose message is particularly appropriate during the last month of the year, the month of Elul: Each of us should see ourselves as half innocent and half guilty, as though our good deeds and our bad deeds completely balance one another. If we then commit one good deed, we tip the scales in our favor!

What a marvelous metaphor! How wonderful a place would our world become if each of us went through life committed to making our next deed a good one.

My late and beloved *Ulpan* teacher in Israel, Sarah Rothbard, used to say, "It is not just a gift for Jews that we created a Day of Atonement (Yom Kippur) and the forty-day period (starting at the beginning of the month of Elul) leading up to it. It is a gift for all humanity.

We each have talents and abilities, and our goal – particularly during the days of Elul – is to ask ourselves, "What particular talents and abilities do I possess? Am I using them only for my own enrichment or enjoyment? Or do I – and if not can I – find ways to use these gifts for the benefit of others.

As I head to Germany to spend time preceding and during the Days of Awe (the period between Rosh Hashanah and

Yom Kippur) and for several weeks thereafter speaking and teaching in synagogues and churches as well as the University of Potsdam School of Theology, it is with the hope that I may use my modest talents to spread knowledge, understanding and appreciation of Jewish ideals and thought in a place that once tried to extirpate the gene pool and practices of our people.

Rabbi Stephen Lewis Fuchs in Edinburgh.

Like my prized Talmud tractate, I was born in 1946. My late father, Leo Fuchs, was arrested on Kristallnacht in the city of Leipzig where he was born and grew up. I look forward with both trepidation and joyful anticipation to delivering the sermon at Leipzig's annual Holocaust commemoration this year.

My presence there I hope will represent the message that the Munich Talmud conveys. In a place which once was ravaged by hatred and destruction, the reaffirmation of the vitality and goodness of Jewish thought are once again encouraged to flourish.

A Most Meaningful Way To Mark Kristallnacht

What a thrill it was to feel the rapt attention and field the thoughtful questions of the group I taught about Cain and Abel in Flensburg last night at the Maria Schmerzhafte Mutter (Mater Dolores) Catholic Church.

American author John Steinbeck, who won the 1962 Nobel Prize for Literature, considered Cain and Abel, "The symbol story of the human soul because it is every person's story." Steinbeck himself considered his most important work to be East Of Eden, an 800-page exegesis of the sixteen-sentence biblical story of Cain and Abel.

Like Cain we have all felt the sting of rejection, and like Cain we have all felt angry and jealous at another's success especially when others judge us as falling short.

But God insists to Cain and to us that we can rule over those feelings of anger and jealousy, and God hopes we do. The final word of Steinbeck's novel quotes God's hope for Cain and for us in the word: תמשל, "You can rule" as in you can overcome the anger and jealousy that you feel.

Yes, we can, but God does not make us.

We have free will and, as painful as the consequences of that free will sometimes are, to take that capacity from humanity would rob our lives of the very meaning and purpose they are supposed to have. We are not marionettes, and God is not a puppeteer.

One of the questions people have asked me most frequently. "How could a good God allow the Holocaust?" The answer is in Cain and Abel, the third story of the very first book of the Torah.

Just as God did not stop Cain, we should not have expected God to stop Hitler. It was up to humanity to do so.

Humans, not God, are responsible for the Holocaust.

It was a privilege to teach these ideas on the eve of Kristallnacht, November 9, 1938, a night that left no doubt as to Hitler's aim, the annihilation of the Jewish people and our religion.

Teaching Torah in Germany proves that he failed!

Kristallnacht is, of course, an occasion of great sadness. I will participate in two commemorative Kristallnacht events in Flensburg tomorrow. To me, though, teaching these vital truths to a Roman Catholic audience is the best Kristallnacht commemoration I can think of.

We cannot undo the past! But teaching and learning about one another in an atmosphere of mutual affirmation and respect is the best way I know to help shape a better future for our children, grandchildren and generations to follow.

I also pledge – and I ask others to pledge with me – to use whatever talents God has given us to bring nearer the time when the world will become the place of which the prophets dreamed, a place when all will live in peace, a place where everyone will sit under his vine and fig tree with none to make us afraid.

Bishop Mussinghoff: An Extraordinary Friend of the Jews

What a privilege it was to witness the mass to celebrate the 75th birthday of the Bishop of Aachen, Heinrich Mussinghoff, whom Vickie and I met three years ago in Jerusalem.

As we entered the cathedral, a reporter with a microphone asked if I would like to wish the bishop a happy birthday. In my greeting I stated why I as an American rabbi was eager to honor Bishop Mussinghoff:

He has been an extraordinary friend of the Jews.

Three years ago, a controversy erupted when a proposed law to ban the practice of infant circumcision in Germany gained significant traction. As Chairman of the Conference of German Bishops, Bishop Mussinghoff eloquently protested that the bill impinged on the religious freedom of Jews and Muslims. He was a major reason for its defeat.

Subsequently, Pope Benedict proposed to reintroduce language in the traditional Good Friday ritual calling for the conversion of the Jews. In response, Bishop Mussinghoff took the extraordinary step of publicly questioning the Pope's decision.

There are not that many Jews in Aachen, so the bishop gained no political capital for his courageous acts. They stem from his firm belief in the legitimacy of the Jewish faith.

Vickie and I will never forget the extraordinary courtesy the bishop showed us. We were his guests at the Bishop's Academy Conference Center for four days. He arranged special tours for us – of the old city of Aachen and of the Charlemagne Cathedral and its treasures – with two expert guides.

On the night before the mass, which was the fiftieth anniversary of Nostra Aetate, the historic church document

Rabbi Fuchs with Bishop Heinrich Mussinghoff.

that formally absolved Jews of responsibility for Jesus' death, the bishop arranged for me to lecture at the academy about my book, which was recently published in German.

For the Thursday afternoon mass, the eighth-century Cathedral overflowed with worshipers. There was a full orchestra and two magnificent and very large choirs. Bishops from all over Germany, and the Cardinal of Cologne joined in the celebration of the mass.

At the reception following the celebration, there was a separate table with kosher food. As I approached it, a determined young nun stopped me and said that the kosher food was reserved for our Jewish guests.

"That would be us," I replied.

"Oh," she said, "Are you Rabbi Fuchs? It seems that you and your wife are the only Jewish guests still here. The Rabbi of Aachen left right after the formal part of the reception."

There was enough kosher food to feed a small Bar Mitzvah party, and so the guardian nun agreed to my suggestion that the non-Jewish guests be welcome to partake of it in addition to the other food being served.

As we left the reception, we picked up a newspaper hot off the press. Its headline proclaimed (in German), "A Bishop for All People!" I could not agree more.

The Church of the Broken Cross

"You must be joking," I said to myself, when, shortly after we arrived in Germany, Pastorin Ursula Sieg informed me that she arranged for me to preach in a church whose Pastor in those days was a Nazi murderer. She was not joking, but I have come to trust Pastor Sieg implicitly, and so I agreed.

Kaltenkirchen is such a beautiful picturesque village, but it is also the site of a former concentration camp where prisoners endured brutal, near starvation conditions. Wealthy neighbors nearby lived their lives in comfort.

Since my visit to the camp, whenever I drove through the region the image of Nazi soldiers with snarling Rottweilers hunting for me flooded my brain and marred the woods' beauty.

The Michaelis-Kirche in Kaltenkirchen, just a few kilometers from the camp is a magnificent 16th century structure that was once the pulpit of Ernst Szymanowski (who Germanized his Polish name to Biberstein). Biberstein was an ardent Hitler supporter who left the church to become a Lt. Colonel in the SS who supervised at least two mass murders that claimed at least 2000 lives. He was tried at Nuremberg for his crimes and sentenced to death by hanging. The sentence was commuted to life in prison, and through pressure exerted by the Lutheran Church, Biberstein was released from prison in 1958 and lived out his life in comfort until he died at 85.

Yesterday I accepted the gracious invitation of Pastorin Martina Dittkrist and became the first rabbi ever to preach in that church. My text was the Exodus passage in which God commanded Moses to carve out two tablets of stone to replace those he smashed, and assured of God's forgiveness, lead the people forward.

I referenced the Midrashic teachings that our ancestors

not only carried the new tablets of the Covenant in the ark, but the smashed broken ones as well. The lesson is that we learn as much or even more from our failures in life as we do from our success.

I also emphasized the difference between the anger of God, which might endure up to four generations, and the love and mercy of God that extends to the thousandth. This was my message. Yes, you must always carry the broken stones that Biberstein represents with you, but you can go forward confident that your atonement is accepted and that your generation does not bear direct responsibility for the sins of the past.

And then I addressed the ghost of Biberstein and said, "Despite your sins, we Jews are still here! Where are you?! Your evil has died and burns in hell, but *Wir sind hier zusammen!* We are here together! We cannot undo the past, and we must always carry its lessons with us. But we do so not to wallow in pity but to shape a better a future."

The symbol of Michaelis-Kirchen in Kaltenkirchen will always be the haunting painting of "The Broken Cross" by Hannelore Golberg that hangs in its reception room as an acknowledgment of the sad chapter in the church's history. As I sat beneath that painting answering questions of a standing-room crowd about our visit and my sermon, the soldiers and Rottweilers were no longer looking for me, and I imagined another cross in the painting standing upright next to the broken one. With Pastorin Dittkrist's, loving guidance may the lessons of both crosses lead the congregation forward on its journey of atonement, reconciliation and faithful service to God.

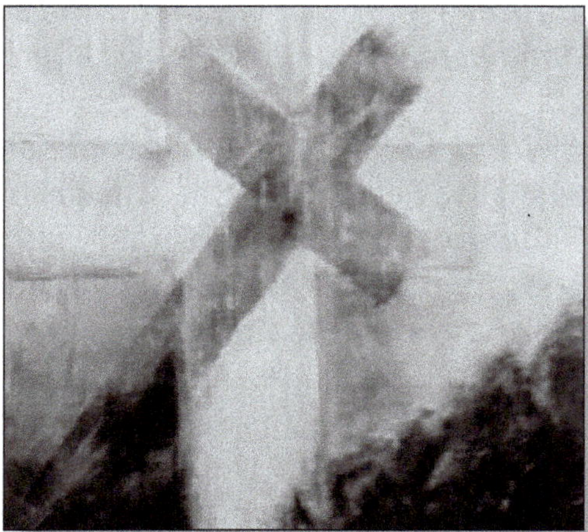

Discussing Psalms at the U. of Hamburg

One of my most gratifying opportunities during our recent trip to Germany was the invitation of Professor Gordon Mitchel to lecture on Psalms to his class of Christian and Muslim students studying to be religious educators at the University of Hamburg.

Psalms are the Jewish people's first prayer book. In it are prayers for every occasion, and they figure prominently in Jewish liturgy to this day.

It was a blessing for me to study Psalms with both Professor Arnold J. Band at Hebrew Union College in Los Angeles and Professor Walter Harrelson, of blessed memory, at Vanderbilt Divinity School. In addition, I study Psalms almost every day.

I began my talk by singing the Hebrew words of Psalm 133. "Behold how good it is for all of us (as brothers and sister) to be together in unity!" Then I slowly pronounced the words, and we all sang it together.

After we sang, I credited the Psalms for enabling me to stand before them that day as a Jew.

Why? By all logic our people should have disappeared when the Second Temple was destroyed in 70 CE.

Before that time our primary form of religious expression was animal sacrifices offered in the Temple in Jerusalem. In those days a hereditary priestly class controlled not only Jewish religious life, but political and economic life as well.

When the Romans destroyed the Temple animal sacrifice and the power of the priesthood also came to an end. Logically, at that point our people should have exited the pages of history like Ammonites, Moabites, Edomites and other ancient peoples.

But we did not because the Pharisees and their heirs, the Sages of the Talmud and Midrash, managed to "re-form" (and I used that word purposely) Jewish life based on (as Rabbi Shimon Ha-Tzaddik expressed it in *Pirke Avot* 1:2) "the study of Torah, prayer, and deeds of kindness and compassion."

With the destruction of The Temple, the already venerable Psalms moved from the periphery to the center of our people's religious life.

For the remainder of my talk I focused on four main points that Psalms express beautifully and effectively:

- Our responsibility as creatures created in the Divine Image to use our talents to create a society marked by justice and righteousness (Psalms 1, 8 and 15).
- The overriding emphasis on using our amazing power to communicate for positive and not negative purposes (Psalms, 19, 34, 51,141).
- The need to cherish our time on earth and use it well, for we never know when it will end (Psalm 90).
- The ability of the Psalms to offer comfort in times of difficulty (Psalm 23).

It was a great thrill for me as Jew to share these universal ideas, to which all of the students could relate, from a particularly Jewish perspective. I appreciate the expressions of gratitude students shared with me.

At the end of the session, Professor Mitchell asked if we might have another round of Psalm 133. It is the only time in my memory that anyone has asked me to sing a second time.

An Unforgettable 10 Weeks in Germany

Vickie and I are still processing the ten amazing and productive weeks we spent in Germany. There were so many highlights.

We owe the trip to the ingenuity and hard work of Pastorin Ursula Sieg of Bad Segeberg. Somehow, after a few meetings with us, Ursula got the idea that we could be useful in a number of different ways in northern Germany this fall. She put together an amazing program and connected all the many dots to make it a reality. In addition, she and her husband Pastor Martin Pommerening hosted us in their home and saw to all the logistics of the trip with warmth and love.

In her role as Director of School Church interaction in her region, Ursula put together a wonderful exhibit for public school children in Neumünster. Its title is, "Coming Home," and it details the life and journey of Vickie's 93-year-old still active artist mother, Stefanie Steinberg. She was born in Breslau, had to flee with her family to Spain from the Nazis when still a child. From there her journey took her to Switzerland, New York, Los Angeles and eventually to San Francisco.

Ursula's creativity and passion for interfaith understanding helped hundreds of students learn about Judaism (for some we were the first live Jews they had ever seen) and the Holocaust in an original and interesting way. We made about ten visits to the school and really felt close to the students and teachers who were involved.

An unexpected surprise came when the Probst of the Lutheran Church of the Bad Segeberg region, Dr. Daniel Havemann, with whom I developed a meaningful friendship, invited me (in his words) to become "the first rabbi to deliver the sermon at the worship service of their

Vickie Fuchs and her mother, Stefanie Steinberg.

annual Synod." It was an honor to do so. In all I spoke at ten different Lutheran Churches, sometimes on very problematic (for Jews) NT texts.

In one of the churches, the one-time pastor was an ardent Nazi who was convicted of atrocities and sentenced to death (later commuted) at Nuremberg. My visit was part of the church's ongoing atonement for Ernst Biberstein's crimes. In the reception room of the church, where there were questions and answers following the service, there hangs a painting of an uprooted cross to symbolize a church gone astray. On my website blog, you might be interested to read more about it in, "The Church of the Broken Cross." It was a very special day.

On Kristallnacht, I was privileged to give three speeches (two in German thanks to Ursula's translation and pronunciation drilling) in Leipzig, the city where my late father was born, grew up, and was arrested on that horrible night, November 9, 1938. My three Kristallnacht addresses in English are also on my web page blog.

We also visited Breslau, and there is interest in bringing

the exhibit about Vickie's mother there as well. It was a thrill for me to watch Vickie's eyes as she took in and processed the many sights from her mother's home city. In Breslau we also received an offer from Jewish community leaders Jan Kirschenbaum and Aleksandra Wilczura to translate and publish *What's in It for Me? Finding Ourselves in Biblical Narratives* into Polish.

Speaking of the book, it was wonderful to visit the huge international book fair in Frankfurt. I was thrilled to see What's in It for Me? among the thousands and thousands of volumes on display. It was also a unique opportunity to learn a bit from the inside about the publishing industry.

Another honor that I treasure is delivering the semester opening lecture based on the book at the University of Potsdam School of Jewish Theology outside of Berlin. The reception my presentation received makes me confident that a similar talk would form the basis of a very meaningful evening or extended program for seminaries, synagogues, churches, mosques or other type of meeting or convention. I would also be excited to offer a mini-mester or similar course on "Genesis-Exodus Stories for Practical Preaching" to seminarians or clergy of all non-fundamentalist denominations.

Of course, all of these activities were based around my role as visiting rabbi during the ten weeks, including the High Holy Day season, at the *Jüdische Gemeinde* in Kiel. There I preached, helped lead services, and led adult study sessions. Thanks to the kindness and flexibility of the community's spiritual leader, Walter Joshua Pannebacker and the wonderful people who comprise the congregation, we felt so very comfortable and at home there.

All in all, it was an amazing time. But now we are home, and I look forward to sharing the experiences I have had and the approach to Torah reflected in *What's in It for Me? Finding Ourselves in Biblical Narratives* with many different groups.

So, Rabbi, What do You *Really* Think About Jesus?

On October 18, I had the privilege to preach at the Church in Neumünster named after the great Protestant theologian, Dietrich Bonhoeffer.

Bonhoeffer was a brilliant student who turned away from a promising career as Professor of Theology to live the teachings of Jesus' life among everyday people as a pastor. He actively opposed Hitler even before he took office and through all the twelve years of his reign.

Opportunities to escape Hitler came to Bonhoeffer from prestigious institutions in New York and London, but like Moses at the Burning Bush, Bonhoeffer could not resist the call to return to Germany despite the danger he faced.

The Nazis executed Dietrich Bonhoeffer at the Flossenbürg concentration camp shortly before the end of the war.

One of his most famous teachings is: To be silent in the face of evil, is to be complicit in evil.

Near the church is a center welcoming and processing thousands of refugees from tyranny in Syria and several other countries. It was my great privilege during my sermon to welcome these Islamic and Christian refugees as my cousins through Abraham.

I noted that on display in the church was the exhibit about Vickie's 94-year-old mother, Stefanie Steinberg, who fled Germany as a 14-year-old refugee in 1936.

"Though she experienced difficult times," I said, addressing the refugees, "her story has a happy ending. I hope and pray that each of yours will too."

Three wonderful pastors ably lead the Dietrich-Bonhoeffer Kirchegemeinde:

Pastor Tobias Gottesleben came to our Simchat Torah service in Bad Segeberg and hosted the study evening at which I spoke two weeks ago. When I preached there, though, he was visiting the church's mission community in the Congo.

Pastorin Ulrike Wohlfahrt led yesterday's service with warmth and deep spiritual feeling. It was a privilege to be there. She led the worship with inspiring respect of the Jewish roots of Christianity, saying, "We have so much to gain by listening to and learning from each other."

Pastorin Isabel Frey-Ranck organizes and coordinates the church's sacred mission of helping the waves of refugees that have come to Neumünster from Syria and several other countries acclimate to their new home.

I see each of these wonderful people as very worthy to lead a church that bears Dietrich Bonhoeffer's name.

During my sermon I noted that Christians often ask me what do I think of Jesus? My answer: It depends on what his followers make of him.

If, as has been the case far too often over the past 2000 years Jesus name has been invoked as justification for persecuting Jews, forcing us to convert, exiling and killing us, then Jesus does not rate high with me.

Of course, Jews will never see Jesus as God or as an object of worship as Christians do.

But when Jesus is the inspiration to feed the hungry, clothe the naked and do the things I see so many churches in Germany do today in his name, I look at him very positively.

And when – as in the case of Dietrich Bonhoeffer – Jesus' example is the impetus to sacrifice position, comfort and even his life to oppose the scourge of Nazism, then I become an admirer of Jesus.

In fact, I become a very big fan indeed.

How a 94-year-old Jewish Woman's Friendship with German Students Changed Them All

My wife Vickie and I were thrilled to learn that our German friends, Pastor Ursula Sieg and her husband Pastor Martin Pommerening, were coming to visit us in America. When we asked if there was anything special, they wanted to do during their visit, they answered, "If it is at all possible, we would like to travel with you to San Francisco to meet Vickie's mother." Although the request surprised us, it was an opportunity we embraced.

For our visit to Germany last fall, Ursula created and curated a remarkable exhibit about the life and travels of Vickie's mother, Stefanie Steinberg. As a young child, Steffi had to leave her native Breslau and flee to Spain with her parents when the Nazis took over Germany. Not long thereafter, they had to flee again, this time to Switzerland, during the Spanish Civil War.

Eventually Steffi made her way to New York, then across the country to Los Angeles, and ultimately to San Francisco. At 94, she is still active as an artist well-known for her paintings, photography, and collages – and for several years now, she has done much of her work on her computer. She lives independently and keeps alert and in great shape by attending lots of lectures and classes and working in her garden. She gave her most recent presentation to the San Francisco Women Artists, of which she is a past president, earlier this year.

When we told her that we planned to spend 10 weeks in Germany last fall, Steffi did not like the idea. Given all she had endured at German hands, her reaction did not surprise us: "Why do you want to go to Germany?"

As the weeks unfolded, it pleased her that her life had become the vehicle for German students to learn about the Holocaust and the basics of Jewish living in a more effective way than books alone could ever teach. Many of these students had never met a living Jew before Vickie and I came to their school.

By the time Vickie and I left Germany, several of the students had sent Steffi very touching emails and voice messages. They wrote that they would do all in their power to ensure such horrors never happened again – to anyone. The bond these German students forged with her has been a healing balm for Steffi.

In addition, Vickie and I had the joy last January of presenting Steffi with an honorary diploma from the Holstenschule in Neumünster, accompanied by a beautiful letter of gratitude from the headmaster. The gesture touched her deeply, especially because the Nazi takeover in Germany forced this erudite and accomplished woman to suspend her formal education years before she could graduate from high school.

For all of these reasons, Steffi was thrilled when she learned that Ursula and Martin were coming to visit her. When the big day came, they embraced like long-time friends. Steffi found more photos to give to her visitors because the exhibit will travel to other schools when Vickie and I return to Germany in September. Then the five of us enjoyed a sumptuous dinner overlooking the Pacific to celebrate Steffi's 94th birthday.

It was a fitting celebration, a wonderful way to honor a remarkable woman whose life and work will always stand to testify against the horror that the Nazis reigned upon Europe. And it was a wonderful way, too, to honor two visionary Lutheran pastors who are making heroic efforts to help Germans confront the horror of their past and replant Jewish life in the land where it once bloomed so beautifully.

Chapter 2

Anti-Semitism

O, The Chimney!

Der Spindel is a quaint café in the center of Bad Segeberg that used to house a wool-processing factory. Because it was an unseasonably warm and sunny late summer day, our host Pastor Martin Pommerening suggested we sit outside.

The setting was pleasant; the conversation was delightful; the food was delicious, and then I looked up and noticed the tall chimney attached to the old wool factory. I shuddered as Israel's Nobel prize-winning poet Nelly Sachs' famous poem seeped into my brain:

O the chimneys
On the ingeniously devised habitations of death
When Israel's body drifted as smoke
Through the air ...

The impulse to run out of the courtyard was strong, but the atmosphere of friendship and the goal of reconciliation, which brought me to Germany, were stronger. I will never be free of evocative stimuli that will bring Holocaust reflections in their wake.

And yet ...

Germany as a nation has done so much to try to atone for the horrors of The Shoah. That does not mean – nor should it – that we shall ever be free of our memories. But can we be free of the anger and antipathy they evoke?

By coming to Germany to teach and speak in synagogues and churches for ten weeks Vickie and I testify that our answer is, "We will try!" It is not always easy, but the effort that has gone into preparing for our trip makes it easier. I can only imagine the hours of time and energy that Pastor Ursula Sieg has devoted to every detail of our visit. The hospitality of Ursula and her husband Martin is so kind and genuine that we shall win this struggle. We shall win it over and over again every time there is a reminder of the horrors of the past.

Each year during The Days of Awe we examine our actions of the past year with a close eye on our shortcomings and the things, which we have done that we regret.

A crucial part of the process is to go to the people we have wronged and ask for their forgiveness. Without these steps our prayers for forgiveness that we shall say on Yom Kippur are meaningless.

And, our tradition teaches, when we sincerely approach someone we have insulted or hurt and ask them to forgive us, they have an obligation to do so. If they refuse us more than twice, the burden of the sin transfers to them!

I cannot speak for other Jews, but I have made the decision to heed and apply this teaching to our people's greatest horror. Germany has asked our forgiveness so many times and in so many ways! As I ask those I have wronged to forgive me, I feel the obligation – even in this case – to forgive as well!

Why?

We cannot undo the past, but the future is ours to shape!

My First Swastika

It was supposed to be just a pleasant walk through the woods by the picturesque River Trave in Bad Segeberg. The moss at river's bottom gave the water a green hue I had never seen before. Tree branches with leaves still green despite the beginning of fall drooped over the bank. We rounded a bend and there it was: a crudely painted swastika scarring the trunk of a tree to our right.

I shuddered! I whirled around as for a fleeting second imagined Nazi soldiers hiding behind the trees waiting to drag me away. But the fear vanished as quickly as it came.

Our host, Pastor Martin Pommerening apologized profusely that we had to see this sight. "But Martin," I responded, "You have nothing to apologize for! You are the antithesis of this swastika. We bask in the warmth and love of your hospitality." *Moreover,* I continued speaking silently to myself. *You and Ursula (his wife Pastorin Ursula Sieg) work tirelessly to learn about Judaism and to educate Germans about Jews. You both have spent countless hours over many months preparing every detail of our ten-week visit. We are partners in a sacred enterprise, and I will not let a random reminder that there are a few who wish to return to the past do anything but strengthen my resolve to work with you toward the goals we both cherish.*

Often people tell me, why don't you just forget the past and look to a brighter future? There are two answers to that question.

First my walk in the woods proved once again as Dionne Warwick and others sang several years ago, "There Is Always Something There to Remind Me!" Even if I wanted to forget, I cannot.

More importantly, though, remembering the past is crucial if we are to avoid repeating the mistakes of the past.

Several people including George Santayana and Winston Churchill, have said, "Those who do not remember history are doomed to repeat it!"

No, forgetting the past is not desirable! Forgiveness without remembering is meaningless. Creating a better future is impossible if we fail to recall the things about the past we are trying to improve.

After we saw the swastika in the woods of Bad Segeberg , Pastor Pommerening immediately called the mayor of the town to tell him what we saw. I am very confident the swastika has already been painted over or will be soon. But I would not the tree chopped down and its stump uprooted in order to pretend that it never happened.

Germany's efforts to atone for the Holocaust and prevent its recurrence are more than admirable. They definitely deserve our forgiveness. But never, *ever,* should we forget!

A Long-Deferred Visit: Auschwitz

To commemorate Yom HaShoah, I share the following reflection of my visit to Auschwitz.

It should always be cold, it seems to me, at Auschwitz, and the sky should always be a dreary gray.

Unless it is a very hot day, I am always cold. It has been that way, it seems to me, since the frigid night in February when my Hamilton College Hockey team played MIT in Boston outdoors.

I was not one of the team's better players (an understatement), and I spent much of the game on the bench. Since then, I have been cold.

And so, as much as any of the horrible sufferings people endured or succumbed to at Auschwitz, I think of the cold.

The thin pieces of rag that inmates wore, and their often-bare feet provided no shield at all against the brutal Polish winter.

It was not cold by normal standards when we visited Auschwitz. But I vowed not to be cold. I wore long johns, knit cap, gloves and four layers of clothing on my upper body.

We came first to the death camp of Birkenau. The stark barrenness and sense that we were in the middle of nowhere combined with the knowledge of what happened there evoked a strong emotional response.

And despite how warmly I dressed and the comparatively mild temperature, I was cold.

Then we made our way to "the main Auschwitz." Tour

buses and crowds greeted us. It seemed we were visiting just another tourist attraction.

The only thing there that I needed to see with my own eyes – given how many other Holocaust museums and memorials I have visited – was the infamous **"ARBEIT MACHT FREI"** sign over the main gate.

It was smaller than I imagined.

But then our friend, Pastor Martin Pommerening pointed out something I had not known.

The B in 'ARBEIT' was upside down.

Instead of the bottom being bigger than the top, the top was bigger than the bottom. I had never noticed.

It was a subtle protest by the workers forced to make the sign against its message. They were telling the world that the sign above the Gate of Auschwitz was a lie.

Then Martin asked if the second letter, the "Bet" ב has any special significance in Judaism.

The rabbis make much, I answered, of the fact that the first word of the Torah, "Beresheet" (In the beginning) begins with "Bet." "Bet" is the first letter of the Hebrew word for "B'racha" which means "blessing," the blessing God charged Abraham and all of us (Genesis 12:2) to make of our lives.

The rabbis also noted that God began Torah with the letter "Bet" because the Bet is closed beneath it, behind it and above it. That teaches that what happens when we are placed beneath the ground, what happened before creation, and so much about God above are beyond our ability to know.

But, the Sages, continued, the Bet is open in front.

That Midrash symbolizes for me the main message I have tried to proclaim in speaking these past three years in synagogues, schools, and churches in Germany:

"We cannot undo the past, but the future is ours to shape."

I could not leave Auschwitz soon enough, and as we drove away, the sun peeked through the clouds as we contemplated the future we wish to shape.

At Dachau

On the infamous "Night of Broken Glass" November 9, 1938, the Nazis unleashed a savage against the Jews of Germany. Leo Fuchs, my father was one of the 30,000 Jewish men arrested in Germany that night and among the 500 arrested in his home city of Leipzig.

Historians called that night, Kristallnacht, or in Germany *Reichspogromnacht*, the clear boundary in time after which no one could any longer doubt Hitler's ultimate plan for Europe's Jews.

That ultimate plan condemned one-third of all the Jews in the world to death. Two-thirds of Europe's Jews and three-fourths of Europe's Rabbis Cantors, Jewish educators and communal leaders perished.

Out of the 18,000 Jews who lived in Leipzig in 1935, Hitler killed 14,000, seven out of every nine.

Upon their arrest on Kristallnacht, Leipzig's captives had to stand in the stream that flows through the city zoo. There Nazi soldiers commanded citizens to spit on them, curse at them, and throw mud on them.

Then they took my father to Dachau where they shaved his head and beat him.

But my father was one of the very fortunate ones. He had an older brother and an uncle already established in the United States. They petitioned Governor Herbert Lehman of New York, a Jew with German roots, and on December 3, 1938, my father was able to sail for New York City.

There he met and married my mother, and my sister Rochelle and I were born. I am very grateful.

I have never visited Dachau, but Dachau visits me often. My father's two older brothers lived into their 80s; my father died at 57.

Yes, I blame Dachau.

If someday I physically go there, these are the words I shall say:

Sometimes silence is the only appropriate response.
When we confront the depths of depravity to which humans can descend,
And the depths of despair that humans can inflict on others,
Slack-jawed silence is the only response that is not flawed.

A Purim Message from Bad Segeberg in 1936

In little more than a month, Purim will be here again. In addition to masks, groggers, and fun-filled Purim spiels, I hope part of our preparation focuses on the vital messages this festival and the Book of Esther, the text that underlies it, send to us today.

The faces in the photo that hangs in the new synagogue in Bad Segeberg haunt me. They seared themselves into my brain the first time I saw it, and they do not let go.

What were these twenty-six souls thinking when – in hiding – they celebrated Purim in 1936? Their eyes and their smiles betray fear as well as their resolve to celebrate the festival with joy.

There are those who demean Purim and the basis for the festival, the Book of Esther. They say:

"It is the only book in the *Tanach* that does not mention God!"

"The story reads a cartoon melodrama. It is obviously a work of fiction."

"I am turned off by the excessive violence described as the Jews take their revenge."

These criticisms notwithstanding, Esther is our prototype story of triumph over forces that have tried to destroy us.

So what if the story is fictionalized and over drawn? It is an inspiring tale of courage.

First of all, there is the courage of Vashti. What a role model she is for women of today who face sexual harassment! When the King wanted her to show her beauty (in the altogether, commentators claim) to his drunken friend, she had the courage to refused. She put her dignity and self-respect above position and power.

Then there is the question of destiny. When Mordecai told Esther to tell the King she was Jewish, she replied, "I can't" No one sees the king without an invitation, and he has not invited me for thirty days.

This is your moment, claimed Mordecai. "Who knows if you did not become queen just for this opportunity that is uniquely yours to stand up for our people?" What a powerful message.

If we look for them, we all have moments when we are in a unique position to make a positive difference. Esther seized her moment. Will we seize ours?

Certainly, the Jews of Bad Segeberg seized their moment in 1936. Their celebration testified that they would not allow the Nazis to cow them.

Each time I stare at the photo I wonder: What befell these brave souls? How many – if any – survived Nazi tyranny and celebrated Purim in freedom at some later time?

Regardless, these brave celebrants are the lineal heirs of Vashti and Esther who placed pride and dignity over expediency and ease.

Few Jews remained in Bad Segeberg when the period of Nazi horror ended. The once proud synagogue in the city crumbled from disuse and was torn down in 1962.

But thanks, in large measure to an influx of Jews from the former Soviet Union, and thanks to the skill and determination of the community's leader Walter Blender who saw to every detail of the construction of the new building, where the 1936 a miracle occurred. Thanks, are also due to the kindhearted support of the Christian community led by Pastors Ursula Sieg and Martin

Pommerening who extended the hospitality of their church to the new Jewish community as it reformed.

Every time I climb the stairs to the sanctuary of Bad Segeberg's Reform (and only) synagogue Mishkan HaTzafon, I look at the 26 brave faces in the photo, and I wish I could thank each and every one.

I have no doubt. Because of the courage of the Jews of Bad Segeberg in 1936 there is Jewish life - a thriving and God willing growing Jewish life - in Bad Segeberg in 2016.

Learning from the Past; Facing the Future

Months ago, when I was invited to speak in Leipzig on Kristallnacht, the invitation filled me with joy. What could be more wonderful? The city where my father was arrested and sent to Dachau has invited me back as its guest to speak at the city's three separate Kristallnacht commemorations. And yet the changes that have occurred since I accepted the invitation six months have tempered my joy with concern.

Anti-Semitism is rising sharply around the world. The aftermath of the Holocaust gave us a respite. Now, the world seems to be going back to business as usual. Questions about the legitimacy of the Jewish state - not this policy or that - but her very right to exist as a Jewish nation don't come just from radical Arab capitals. They come from England, France, Belgium, Holland, Scandinavia and even here in Germany now and then.

Anti-Semitic attacks on Jewish institutions hardly make the general news anymore, but they are becoming more common. In Europe anti-Semitic violence is such a pervasive threat that if you wish to visit a synagogue, you had best have a reservation in advance or the locked and guarded building is likely to be off limits.

How should we respond to such existential concerns?

One Yom Kippur a congregation responded to the plea of Rabbi Meir of Apt to repent by bursting into tears. After enduring the sobbing for two hours, the rabbi addressed his congregation saying: "Jews, I don't want you to turn to God with tears and sadness. I want you to turn to God with joy and hope." (S. Y. Agnon, *Days of Awe,* page 210)

Yes, we live in troubled times. Israel is besieged from every corner of the world, and Anti-Semitism is sprouting anew even at times here in Germany where it is forbidden by law.

Are we to succumb to despair? No, as the Rabbi of Apt advised, our task is to find joy, wherever we can and do our very best to live up to God's hopes for us, and trust that if we do, God will see us through the perils in our path as God promised Abraham so long ago.

This summer, Israel's long period of quiet exploded into a horrible war. Certainly, it was neither a lasting military nor a moral victory for Israel.

In the grief and of disappointment, over the loss of life both of Israelis and of innocent Palestinians we need perspective. I find it here in Germany. Despite occasional Anti-Semitic expressions, I see daily reminders of where we Jews were just decades ago, and how far we have come.

Currently, the Holstenschule in Neumünster has a beautiful exhibit based on the life of my wife's 93-year-old artist mother, Stefanie Steinberg. Her maiden name is Apt, and maybe the hope and joy with which she lives, despite what she endured, was taught to her forbears by the famous Rabbi Meir of Apt, whom I quote above.

The Neumünster exhibit allows students a wonderful opportunity to learn of her remarkable life journey from Breslau to Spain, to Switzerland to New York to Los Angeles and eventually to San Francisco where she still lives independently and recently gave a marvelous talk to the San Francisco Women's Artists in which she has been active for over half a century. The ingenious exhibit in Neumünster, designed by Lutheran Pastor Ursula Sieg educates students and members of the public who visit not just about the horrors of the Holocaust but about Jewish thought, history and practice as well.

Just last week I spoke at the University of Potsdam to open the semester of the School of Jewish Theology and to rabbinical students at the Abraham Geiger College in Berlin. Both of these institutions offer their tutelage to our future professionals in Europe at government expense.

Can this be Germany?

As Jews we have many roles to play in this world. We are not just a beleaguered country that became a State in 1948. We are not just congregations - in North America and around the world - concerned for our fiscal and programmatic futures. And we are certainly not just those whose past is tied to the destruction of European Jewry during World War II.

No, we are a people with a 4000-year-old Covenant with God, a Covenant that calls on us to (as God called on Abraham and Sarah: Be a blessing in the lives that we lead (Genesis 12:2) and to follow as best we can God's teachings and to be worthy of them (Genesis 17:1). Our Covenant with God also calls us to use every ounce of our talent to try to create in our homes, in our neighborhoods, in our synagogue, in our nation, in Israel, and in our world a just, caring, compassionate society built on the biblical ideals - of Tzedakah and Mishpat - of righteousness and justice (Genesis 18:19).

Although I have real concerns as I return to the city of my father's birth and upbringing, I will certainly be aware that the Leipzig to which I return is very different than the Leipzig my father left. Buoyed by the reality of today, I will return to Leipzig to proclaim with the joy and hope Rabbi Meir of Apt recommends.

Although we can never undo the past, we can learn its lessons and build a better future - a future marked by righteousness and justice - for ourselves our children and the generations to come.

Paris: Hope in the Face of Terror

The Probst of the Lutheran Churches of Bad Segeberg, Dr. Daniel Havemann, has been incredibly gracious, kind and welcoming to Vickie and me. He invited me to preach the first sermon I delivered in Germany in 2014 in the historic *Marien* Cathedral in Bad Segeberg. This year he invited me to preach at the end of my visit. It is as though Dr. Havemann's friendship and authority created a protective and comforting bracket around our extended stays in Germany.

Our joy, of course, paled against the anger and sadness caused by the horrific attacks on Paris.

Pundits are telling us to accustom ourselves to this new reality of dozens of people mercilessly murdered by savage forces in the name of religion.

I refuse to do so.

Fittingly, the text about which Dr. Havemann requested I preach – long before the Paris event – was the destruction of Sodom and Gomorrah.

No text could have been more fitting.

Our Rabbinic Sages probably could not have imagined the magnitude of the attack on Paris. They had no concept of mass coordinated assaults on innocent civilians in sports stadiums and theaters with sub-machine guns and other weapons of mass destruction.

But because the Torah tells us that Sodom and Gomorrah were so wicked that The Eternal One destroyed them, our Sages' fertile minds gave us graphic pictures of how depraved those societies were.

Three Midrashim

In Sodom, visitors had one-size beds. If the guest was

too tall, they would lop of his legs at the point where he or she would fit. If the person was too short for the bed, they stretched him until he fit (Babylonian Talmud, Sanhedrin 109B).

Another Midrash tells of one of Lot's daughters who violated a law of the city against feeding the poor. In Sodom that was a capital crime, and Lot's daughter cried out to the Eternal One to save her from the punishment of being burned alive for her offense (Pike d'Rabbi Eliezer 25; Beresheet Rabbah 49:6).

There was also a law in Sodom against welcoming guests into one's home. Of course, the Torah tells us that Lot violated this law by not only welcoming guests but also protecting them from the assault of an angry mob outside.

Lot's wife, though, the Midrash teaches, wanted to betray her husband to the authorities of Sodom. She went to neighbors to borrow salt because, she said, her husband wanted to offer a tasty meal to her guests. That is the reason, the Midrash concludes, that Lot's wife was eventually turned into a pillar of salt (Beresheet Rabbah, 51:5; 50:4).

Yes, the depravity of Sodom parallels the depravity of those who attacked Paris. Anger and rage are appropriate responses, but despair is not.

Our tradition forbids us to abandon hope that things can be better. It is for that reason that Israel's national anthem is called, "התקוה, Ha-Tikvah, The Hope."

Another story (that I first heard from Ambassador David Saperstein when he spoke at the congregation I served, Temple Isaiah in Columbia MD in the late 70s) makes this point:

Once there was a man who traveled to Sodom every day asking the people there to repent their evil ways and to change. The scoffed at him and mocked him. But every day he would return with the same message of repentance.

When he returned home his wife and family chided him, "Why do you go down there day after day? Don't you know those people will never change and become like you?"

"You may be right," the man would answer. "Perhaps those people will never change and become like me. But I must go down there – day after day – so that God forbid, I do not become like them."

And so...

Even in the face of wickedness that defies description, we must never abandon hope.

We must continue to dream of and work – each in our own small ways – to bring nearer the day of which the prophets dreamed when:

"They shall not hurt or destroy in all My holy mountain for the earth shall be filled with the knowledge of the Eternal One as the seabed is covered by water" (Isaiah 11:9).

And all shall sit under their vines and under their fig trees with none to make them afraid" (Micah 4:4).

Back to Kaltenkirchen

Kaltenkirchen was one of the first places Vickie and I visited on our first extended trip to Germany in 2014.

Then we visited a tiny Concentration Camp site and noted the stately houses just across the street where people lived their lives and said nothing.

Two weeks later I became the first rabbi to deliver a sermon at Michaeliskirche in that village. Their wonderful Pastor, Martina Dittkrist was eager for me to do so because the church's history was marred by a previous Pastor, Ernst Biberstein, who served during the thirties. Biberstein left the church and became a Nazi officer who was convicted of atrocity war crimes at the Nuremberg Tribunal and held responsible for the deaths of 2,000-3,000 Jews.

In the Social Hall of the church, a painting by Hannelore Golberg symbolizes the impact of Biberstein's ministry on the church. It depicts a cross that is uprooted from the ground and tilted on its side. There is also a tasteful plaque in the main sanctuary expressing the church's sorrow that they had once trusted such a man as their spiritual guide. I named a previous essay about that experience, "The Church of the Broken Cross."

That sermon was the first time that I used what has become in many speeches in Germany since, my catch phrase:

We cannot undo the past, but the future is ours to shape.

It was a gratifying but gut-wrenching experience!

Those words could also describe our recent visit to the Gymnasium Kaltenkirchen.

There we met for 90 minutes with a group of combined classes totaling some 80 students. They listened with rapt attention – some had tears in their eyes – as Vickie spoke about her mother and I spoke about my father. We emphasized how her mother and my father were among the truly lucky ones to escape the inferno before it engulfed Europe's Jews. Still both Vickie's mother and my father suffered, and it is important for students to understand their history.

Although the message of these two experiences was similar, our mood in the respective settings was quite different.

During the church service people looked back and realized the horror of the era with genuine regret. There was visible emotion, but most of those in the congregation had lived most of their lives.

By contrast, the teenagers at the Gymnasium present a different picture. They are part of the group that will shape the future of Germany and Europe.

We left with a feeling of great hope. They seemed as determined as any group we have ever seen to ensure that they want to create a better future for themselves, their children, grandchildren and generations to come.

Their responses to the lessons we taught made us very glad that we were there.

To Welcome the Stranger

Thoughts shared at Kirchengemeinde, Schulensee, Germany, October 9, 2016 (In Honor of Rabbi (Dr.) Ferenć Raj, who has exemplified these ideals throughout his distinguished career).

We Jews are incredibly proud of our Torah! But we never claim that Torah was history's first Code of Law. There are several that came before. The Code of Hammurabi was the most famous.

But we do claim that Torah was the first code to grant equal protection under the law to the non-citizen. "You shall not oppress the stranger for you were strangers in the land of Egypt."

It may surprise you to know that this idea, so beautifully read for us this morning, does not appear just once in our Torah nor even twice.

The Torah emphasizes this crucial revolution in human thinking no fewer than 36 times. No other commandment appears so frequently.

We find the roots of this commandment in the stories about the man we consider the first Jew, Abraham. Our Torah teaches that God – to see the world become more just, caring and compassionate – made a Covenant with Abraham and all of us who see ourselves as his descendants.

In the Covenant, God promised:

- To protect Abraham
- Give him the progeny he desperately craved
- Make him and his seed a permanent people. (After 4,000 years, we are still here. That is permanent, is it not, even by European standards?)

- Finally, God promised us that tiny sliver of land in the Middle East that is Israel today.

But a covenant is not just a unilateral promise. It is a binding agreement.

In exchange for these rewards, God charged Abraham and all of us:

- To be a blessing (Genesis 12:2).
- To walk in God's ways and live up to God's teachings (Genesis 17:1).
- To fill the world and teach his descendants - again, that is all of us - with צדקה ומשפט (*Tzedakah u'mishpat*), "righteousness and justice" (Genesis 18:19).

As the Torah teaches (Genesis 18:1-8) Abraham rushed out into the desert to greet three strangers. He brought them into his tent, helped them wash, and then served them a sumptuous meal.

Our Midrashic tradition expands the lesson of this story. We read that Abraham's tent had an opening on all four of its sides so that he would see all who approached his tent from any direction. Then he would rush out into the desert to welcome them in the way we read of his welcome this morning.

Another legend tells that once an old man was wandering toward his tent, and Abraham, as was his custom, ran out to greet him. He ushered him into his tent, helped him was and served him a delicious meal in the same manner that he welcomed the three men in this morning's reading.

After the man finished dining, though, he took an idol out of his sack and began to worship it.

Abraham was furious that the man would profane his tent with such blasphemy.

He screamed at the man in rage, picked him up bodily and through him, his idol and his sack out into the desert.

Then he heard the voice of God.

"Abraham, Abraham! I have put up with that man and his idol worship for 75 years! Could you not have tolerated him for even a single night?"

Ashamed, Abraham ran out into the cold desert night, caught up with the man, apologized profusely and implored him to return to his tent.

So, what does this teach us?

Germany has done more than any country to welcome refugees from upheaval in foreign lands, particularly in Syria. She has learned from the horrible period of Nazi rule. Her efforts have been exemplary, but no one can deny that the presence of people who appear different and have different customs makes some people uneasy.

But our biblical mandate is clear!

If we truly consider ourselves descendants of Abraham, we must – even if it is not always convenient – go out of our way to bring them into our tent as they recover from the ravages of war, displacement and great loss.

Yes, if we would honor the example of Abraham, we must welcome those who seek asylum in our midst and, to paraphrase the prophet Micah, settle them under their new vines and fig trees and do our utmost to see that none shall make them afraid (Micah 4:4).

Chapter 3

Leipzig

Letter to my Father…Leipzig Zoo

The Union for Reform Judaism has published the letter I wrote to the memory of my father and read last year in the Leipzig Zoo on Kristallnacht. This year I accepted the invitation to present it at the Kristallnacht commemoration of the Kirchengemeinde St. Nikolai in Flensburg. Vickie also spoke during the service about her mother's journey from Breslau to Spain, to Switzerland, to New York and eventually to Los Angeles and San Francisco. She was wonderful!

The music featuring famous Yiddish songs and "Jerusalem of Gold" provided by the Kinder-und Judendchor under the direction of Gerald Jensen and the organist, Michael Mages was absolutely amazing.

I am especially grateful to Pastor Thomas Bornemann for the care and devotion which went into the planning of the commemoration and to Barbar Winkler who read a German translation of my letter after I shared the text found in English below.

By Rabbi Stephen Lewis Fuchs, 11/09/2015

Is this the place? Is this where they took you, my precious father, on that horrible night?

Is this the place where they spit on you, cursed you, threw mud on you, and reviled you for the crime of being a Jew?

I am so thankful, my father, that you made it out of Kristallnacht – and out of Germany – alive. I am thankful that Uncle Allie and Uncle Morris, who spent the best years of their lives in this city, could get you out and bring you to New York. I am thankful that you met my mother and that my sister and I could be born. I am thankful that you raised us as proud Jews, and I hope you are proud that I am standing here today. But I cannot be sure.

I cannot be sure because you never, ever spoke to me of the night I have come to this place to commemorate.

You spared me the trauma that – as I now know – scarred you. But I thank you, for though you were scarred, you persevered, you and Mother created a warm, loving Jewish home for Rochelle and me.

You taught us of our ancestor, Rabbi Zvi Hirsch Kalischer, the first Orthodox rabbi to encourage Jews to settle in the Land of Israel in fulfillment of their sacred Covenant with God.

You taught us of your father, Hirsch Wolf Fuchs, who was murdered at the beginning of World War I, leaving you as a baby to grow up without a father to teach you the things only a father can teach.

But we were blessed to have you.

You told me one story that I recall now: When you were born, your parents named you Leo Eliezer Fuchs. Eliezer means "God is my help," but the German government – even in 1913 – informed your parents that Eliezer was not an acceptable name for a German boy, and so you became Leo Elias Fuchs.

Your silent protest was to never – ever – use your middle name. It was a subtle protest, but it was not lost on me, and so when your oldest grandson came into the world, my wife Victoria and I proudly named him Leo Eliezer Fuchs in your memory.

I am here today with Vickie, whom you would have adored, but you never got to meet her. As we stand in this place today, I fight back tears – but I did not come here only to weep.

Today, my precious father, we have come to a different Germany than the one you left, in the words of the Prophet Zechariah, like, "a brand plucked from the fire!" (Zechariah 3:2).

Yes, Dad, Vickie and I have come to a Germany that is very different.

We have come to Germany as welcome guests in the home of German pastors who have planned for months to make our visit comfortable and productive.

We have come to a Germany where anti-Semitic speech and actions are forbidden.

We have come to a Germany where rabbis, cantors, and Jewish professionals from all Europe learn and train at government expense.

We have come to a Germany that has paid billions in reparations to Israel and to families like ours, whose members suffered the ravages of the Shoah.

To this land of those who perpetrated the greatest horror that I can imagine, I come to say: Remember!

And indeed, I shall remember.

I shall remember the horror as long as there is breath in my body, and my children – and, I pray, my grandchildren and those who come after – will remember as well.

But I also forgive.

I forgive because Germany has asked for forgiveness so many times and in so many ways. I forgive because of all that Germany has done to repent the horror of the Nazi era.

I forgive.

Speaking for myself and my family alone (for that is as far as my influence extends), I feel called to say, as God said to the children of Israel long ago, "I forgive as you have asked!" (Numbers 14:20).

I accept their *Teshuvah*, their repentance. I forgive, and I join hands with all who stand with us here and with all of those around the world who commemorate this day, seared into memory.

Why I Have Come to Leipzig

This is where my father became Bar Mitzvah in February 1926.

This is my third visit to the city where my father was born, grew up and where (as three sterling dishes that I treasure attest) he won citywide doubles championships in table tennis in 1929, 1930 and 1933, the very year Hitler came to power.

On the occasion of my first visit in 1982 I was turned away at the East German border crossing, Oebesvelde, when I naively told the passport inspector that I was a rabbi on my way to Leipzig to visit the city of my father's youth. Only after a day-long detour to Berlin – where I reinvented myself as an art teacher eager to visit Leipzig's famous museums – did I receive a visa. All during my visit I prayed that no one would ask me anything about art!

At that time the Jewish communal headquarters was a tiny, dusty, hard to find and cramped suite of offices that I reached by climbing a creaky, narrow staircase. The head of the community informed me at the time that 67 Jews lived in Leipzig. Learning that number chilled me to my very core. In 1935 there were 18,000 Jews in Leipzig; 14,000 of them perished in the Shoah.

By contrast, my visit in 2011 introduced me to a lovely refurbished synagogue, spacious offices and a guided tour of the places where my relatives had lived. I was accompanied by the young rabbi of Leipzig's Jewish community, which had been revitalized by the arrival of hundreds of Russian immigrants.

Last winter when Pastorin Ursula Sieg first proposed that Vickie and I come to Germany to speak in synagogues, School, the University of Potsdam and here today, it seemed a natural step in the remarkable progress Germany has made to atone for the horrors of the Hitler era. Indeed, in

2011 and 2012, in my capacity as President of the World Union for Progressive Judaism, I was honored to sign papers that led to the establishment of the School of Jewish Theology at the University of Potsdam. These agreements paved the way for the formal arrangements for the German government to fully fund the German students studying Judaic subject including those studying to be rabbis.

In the last months, though, anti-Semitism has arisen forcefully in many places in Europe. Even here in Germany, where law bars public expressions of anti-Semitism, we have seen the simmering of overt hatred of Jews once again. With these developments, the entire timbre of my visit has changed. When Israel responded forcefully to Hamas' attacks on its civilians, much of the world blamed Israel. This totally inappropriate reaction to Israel's thankfully successful efforts to protect its citizens from the terror of those who dedicate themselves to her destruction - gives credence once again to the notion that we Jews are as the Moabite seer Balaam proclaimed long ago, "a people that dwells alone" (Numbers 23:9).

Practically overnight, we learned that our generation of Jews is not exempt from Balaam's prophecy. As the day of our departure from the United States drew near, some friends and family members voiced reasonable concern about our coming to Germany. But my family and I are here: my wife, Victoria, my cousin Irene, whose parents both were born and raised in Leipzig, her partner Joe Azizazoff, and our son, Leo Fuchs, named for my father who was arrested here and sent to Dachau 76 years ago today!

We have come with joy and gratitude for your invitation. After nearly two months in this country, I know that so many Germans are eager to learn about our faith, our history and our way of life. I am here because I believe, as did Anne Frank, in the essential goodness of humankind. I am here because, though we cannot undo the past, the future is ours to shape!

Thomaskirche Kristallnacht Speech

It is a great honor for me to speak in this historic church to commemorate this horrific night 76 years ago. I am so very grateful to Pastorin Brita Taddiken of the Thomaskirche and to Pastor Timotheus Arndt for the invitation. I also want to express my eternal gratitude to Pastorin Ursula Sieg and Pastor Martin Pommerening for both welcoming Vickie and me into their home and for the endless hours each has put in to make our ten-week stay in Germany so productive and meaningful.

I first found out what happened on this night in 1938 when I began my graduate studies to become a rabbi at the Hebrew Union College in Los Angeles. At the opening convocation the then dean and later President of the College, Rabbi Alfred Gottschalk, of blessed memory, told of how as an eight-year-old child in the town of Oberwesel, he watched his grandfather wade into the river Rhine to save charred scraps of Torah scrolls thrown by the Nazis from his burning synagogue.

As my train pulled into Leipzig's huge station, I realized that my first glimpse of the city was probably my father's last as he traveled on a different kind of train to Dachau after his arrest on Kristallnacht, November 9, 1938.

I picked up a detailed city map at the information center to try to find the street and apartment where my father had grown up. I also sought the location of the city zoo.

Why the zoo? The eyewitness report on Kristallnacht by David H. Buffum, American consul in Leipzig, reveals: "Jewish dwellings were smashed into, and the contents looted ... An eighteen-year-old boy was hurled from a three-story window to land with both legs broken ... three synagogues were fired simultaneously by incendiary bombs, and many Jews were rounded up and thrown into the stream that flows through the city zoo. SS men commanded horrified spectators to spit, jeer, and defile them with mud."

When I arrived at the entrance to the zoo, it was 6:45 p.m. The gatekeeper said I was too late. "The zoo closes at seven."

"It is all right," I answered, as I handed over the entrance fee. "I only need to go in for a few minutes." The gatekeeper protested, but I persisted until she finally let me pass.

In a few minutes I was standing before the stream. Tears came to my eyes as I heard myself asking out loud, "Is this where they took you, Papa? Did those bastards spit on you... did they throw mud on you?" Then, as if in retaliation, I spit into the water from a bridge that straddles the stream.

The next morning, I found the office of the Leipzig Jewish community. The elderly lady who answered the door explained that the head of the community was out but would be back later. I explained to her that my father grew up in Leipzig. She pulled down a dusty ledger and opened it to the F's. I quickly found the family listing.

While we were talking, the leader of the community walked in. I explained who I was and why I was there. He was warm, friendly, and clearly pleased that I had come.

I asked him, "How many Jews live in Leipzig?"

"Sixty-seven," he answered.

"And how many lived here," I continued, "when the Jewish population was at its peak?"

"In 1935," he responded, "Eighteen thousand Jews lived in Leipzig."

"How many perished during the Holocaust?" I asked.

"Fourteen thousand," he replied.

The twelve-hour train ride to Amsterdam gave me plenty of time to digest my experiences in Leipzig. I thought, of course, of my father. After Kristallnacht, the Nazis took him to Dachau where they shaved his head, interrogated him, and abused him.

But Leo Fuchs was one of the lucky ones. Because he

had relatives already in the United States, and because his visas were complete and in order, the American consulate secured his release after only a few days.

He never spoke of any of this to me, but I know the trauma's effect never left him. In the spring of 1969 my father fell gravely ill. I flew home to New Jersey from my rabbinical studies in Los Angeles to be with him. I shall never forget my feelings of helplessness when I entered the hospital room, and my father in a semi-comatose state did not recognize me.

I stood there and shuddered as he began shouting in German – which he never spoke at home – that the guards should stop beating him! He had repressed those memories for more than 30 years.

And they were – by and large – good years! In this country my father found love and raised a family. But I – perhaps irrationally – blame the Nazis for shortening his life and depriving me of sharing my greatest joys with him: My ordination as a rabbi, my marriage to Vickie, and our children and our grandchildren.

Why do I say this? My father died at age 57. His older brothers who left Germany before Kristallnacht lived well into their 80s.

Our children! They are our people's answer to Hitler's madness. For us Jews each new life represents a young sapling planted not only to bring joy to a family but also to revitalize a once verdant forest ravaged by fire, by smoke, and by gas.

The word, "genocide," which we throw around so loosely today, came into our vocabulary so that we could attempt to define what Hitler tried to do: to extirpate the gene pool of our people.

And so, we command ourselves: זכור Remember! But if we only remember to wallow in our sorrow, then we waste our time and our tears. We must remember what was so that we can make what will be better.

People ask me all the time. "How could God allow the Holocaust?" I answer that God gave human beings free will and placed us in charge of and responsible for this world. Without free will life would have no meaning. We human beings would be mere puppets on a string or actors following a script from which we could not deviate.

God yearns for us to create a world of justice and compassion, but God does not do it for us. When we fail, it is our failure, not God's. When we fail, I believe God weeps with us and for us.

As I walked away from the stream that flows through the Leipzig zoo, I wandered past a den of timber wolves in a natural enclosure and beheld a truly wondrous site. A mother wolf stood stark still, while two suckling cubs nursed blissfully at her breasts.

At first, I thought it so incongruous to see such an exquisite glimpse of nature's harmony in a place that represented to me only discord and destruction. Yet, that is the image that lingered in my mind during the long train ride back to Amsterdam. My mind's eye kept returning from the vision of violence, hatred, and pain to the peaceful, pastoral scene of wolf cubs drawing sustenance and strength from their mother.

I know that the Nazis and neo-Nazis use the wolf as a symbol. That is a perversion! Wolves don't kill because of ideology or cruelty – only to survive.

The Leipzig zoo will always represent for me the horrible evil of which humanity is capable. The wolves, though, will always represent harmony God wants us to create in this world.

On Yom Kippur we read in our synagogues one of the Torah's most important texts: "See I have set before you life and goodness, death and evil" (Dt. 30:15). The choice is ours, but God exhorts us: "Choose life that you and your offspring may live" (Dt. 30:19).

No, the question is not, *Where was God during the Holocaust?* The question is, *Where was humanity?*

We cannot change the past, but we can learn from it. We know too well that we can choose death, but God hopes our past will strengthen us as we face the future.

Yes, we can choose death, but God hopes
That the pain we relive this night will give us the courage
To clothe the naked,
Feed the hungry,
Teach the unlettered,
Foster understanding among all people,
And use the vast talents – with which God has blessed us –
To choose life, and
To forge a world of justice, caring, compassion and peace!

And then, at last, we will have the world of which the prophets dreamed when they said (Isaiah 11:9 and Micah 4:4):

> *They shall not hurt nor destroy in all My holy mountain, for the earth will be filled with the knowledge of the Eternal One as the seabed is covered by water ... and all shall sit under their vines and under their fig trees and none shall make them afraid!*

Amen.

Was it a Miracle?

And Elijah heard the voice of God: Not in a whirlwind, not in an earthquake, not in a fire, but "in the still small voice of calm" (I Kings 19:12).

Two years ago, I stood in the pulpit of the Thomaskirche (Bach Cathedral) in Leipzig and told of my father's arrest in that city on Reich's Pogromnacht (Kristallnacht) on November 9, 1938. I told of how the German soldiers rounded up Leipzig's Jews and made them stand in the stream that flows through the city zoo. I told how the Nazis commanded citizens to curse the Jews, spit on them and throw mud at them. I spoke of how I imagined my father in that stream.

I posted my message on my website blog, and in the days that followed I received a number of heartfelt comments about it.

But I have received no comments about that message since then ... until two years later, the day before I was to preach in the Thomaskirche again. In the middle of the night I woke up and felt compelled to check my email. There was a response to my Thomaskirche post from two years ago.

The message I received touched my soul! It came from an American artist living in Leipzig named, to my amazement, Stephen Lewis, who shared this story with me:

When just by chance I came across your blog post, "Thomaskirche Kristallnacht Speech: A Trip I had to Make," I read it, and now feel I must do my best to tell you a story told to me by a dear friend that I briefly knew for a few years before he died. I am a painter and not the best with words but hope to be able to bring it across to you in the most sincere way.

One day shortly after moving my art studio into an

old storefront on Arthur Hoffmann Str. in Leipzig, I was welcomed to the building by a kind elderly couple named the Bernstein's. They lived on the first floor above my studio. My German was very poor and the Bernstein's spoke only a few words of English but they told me many stories about their families, the war, and the GDR. The stories started out easy and simple and were often followed by questions for me asking if I had known about such events. Herr Bernstein would visit me while I was painting, but I was soon helping them carry groceries or delivering coal to them from their basement. These chores were always followed by sweet coffee in their kitchen and occasionally a session of show and tell.

As time went on, the stories became deeper and it seemed to me as though they had not been told before.

Once, while Frau Bernstein was out having her hair done, Herr Bernstein told me about a bright young man that was his mate, his friend, someone whom he quite adored. They were pals. He told me about the boy's family and then mentioned they were Jewish.

Herr Bernstein froze standing at the edge of the table with his age-worn hands clenching the sides of the tabletop and he began to cry.

I could see him relive the moment when as a young man he was ordered to go to the Leipzig Zoo where many Jews were being held in a place where you could look down into the space from above.

Herr Bernstein wanted me to understand this story. It was important. He was confessing of his disgust for the Nazis and failure to do the right thing. He explained that as he went over to see what was going on, he went by a group of German soldiers and looked down in the pit. He said he was shocked to see all of the people. He could not believe it. He was ashamed and horrified. Soldiers were yelling down at them, spitting on them, one soldier even urinated on them from above.

Herr Bernstein was outraged and tried to shame the soldier to stop. Herr Bernstein was struck and knocked to the ground.

With tears running down his face he looked at me and pointed to the kitchen floor. He sobbed and told me he saw his school time friend down in the pit. He was so ashamed to confess he was not able to help his friend. That young man looked up at him and recognized Herr Bernstein. He could see Herr Bernstein being kicked and spit on. He was silenced. Mr. Bernstein was there, saw the horror, but was not able to save his friend.

I share this story with you not to make light of your experience visiting the Zoo or to try to make excuses for the Germans.

After reading your account of the captured Jews at the Zoo, I thought that if you knew about how at least one person tried stop the madness, how the victims might have witnessed how at least one German young man knew what was happening was wrong and tried to stop the soldiers, that this might mean that God was at work during this terrible and hopeless event.

Herr Bernstein said he could see strength in his friend's eyes looking up at him. He could still see him and was crushed while telling me about this event.

The peculiar reason that I came across your blog – and somehow this article – is because you and I share the same name.

I wish you well.

Sincerely, Stephen Lewis

A Jewish legend that I love teaches: "When the living think of the dead, the dead who are in paradise know they are loved and they rejoice." *

After I shared a summary of this story with the worshipers, and announced with joy that Stephen Lewis, the artist, was in attendance, I said:

"Herr Bernstein, I stand here tonight with the hope that you rejoice in the knowledge that we remember and cherish your remarkable act of courageous resistance to Nazi terror."

For Jews, Elijah the Prophet represents the hope that one day we will have the world of peace and harmony that God has yearned for humans to create.

For that reason there are more Jewish stories and legends about Elijah than any other biblical character. **

One of my favorites tells that because of his righteousness, the third century Sage Rabbi Joshua ben Levi had the privilege of visits by the prophet.

One day the rabbi asked Elijah, "When will the Messiah come to redeem the world?"

"Today," Elijah answered.

Rabbi Joshua waited expectantly the whole day, but he saw no Messiah.

---

* Though I have tried, I cannot trace the source of that particular legend further back than Noah Gordon's wonderful 1964 novel, *The Rabbi.* I first read that novel when I was 18 years old. That is long enough for me to quote, with gratitude to Mr. Gordon, snippets of it as authentic Jewish folklore.

** Think of it, Moses is the subject of four of the five books of the Torah. Elijah stories only take up 15 pages of text in the First Book of Kings. Yet we have far more rabbinic legends and stories about Elijah than about Moses.

When Elijah visited him again that evening, the rabbi asked, "Why didn't the Messiah come?"
"He is here," Elijah answered.
"Where," the rabbi asked?
"You can find him on the outskirts of town, among the outcasts, among the lepers."
"How will I know which one he is," the rabbi asked?
"He is the one who changes the bandages of the lepers," Elijah answered. "He changes them one by one."

I continued:

We can no longer wait for a grand sweeping act of redemption. We must each do what we can – one by one – to make the world better.

In the Bible, Elijah perceived God's will not in a whirlwind, not in an earthquake and not in a fire, but in "a still small voice" (I Kings 19:12).
The still small voice speaks to all of us from time to time. Though the price he paid was very dear, Herr Bernstein heeded it when it spoke to him.

How will we respond when it speaks to us?

Return to the Leipzig Zoo

The other day, I went back to the Leipzig zoo.

The Zoo was only a fraction of its present size when I last visited it in 1982. Then I had to lie to enter East Germany.

When the train I was on back then came to the tiny border crossing at Oebisfelde, the guard asked me why I wanted to go to Leipzig.

Naively I answered, "My father was born and grew up in Leipzig. He lived here until he was arrested on Kristallnacht. I am a rabbi, and I want to see where he lived."

As I spoke, I could see the guard's face harden. "You cannot enter the country. You must take a train (five hours in the complete opposite direction) to Berlin and ask for a visa. They will decide there, if you can enter or not."

In Berlin I told the border official that I was an art teacher (praying all the while he would not ask me anything about art) who wanted to see Leipzig's famous museums. I received a thirty-six-hour visa.

When I finally got to Leipzig, I went straight to the zoo just to stand at the stream in which the Nazis forced Jews to wade on Kristallnacht.

I envisioned my father standing in that stream while citizens obeyed the Nazi soldiers' commands to spit, jeer, and throw mud at them.

In 1982 I poured out my anger and my bittiness, and I spit into the stream in retaliation. But as I walked toward the zoo's exit, a remarkable sight transfixed me. A mother wolf stood stark still while her baby nursed.

How, I wondered, could a scene of such peace and tranquility exist in a place that represented such horror to me?

On that day I decided to embrace the message of those

wolves. Although the wolf once symbolized Nazi ferocity, these wolves represented peace and harmony to me. They assuaged my anger with hope that the future could be better than the past.

And things are better.

This year I came to Leipzig to speak at *Kabbalat Shabbat* on Friday evening in the synagogue, on Sunday in a Lutheran church, on Monday afternoon to a group of Protestant youth, and later that evening at a Catholic center about the German edition of my book: What's In it for Me? Finding Ourselves in Biblical Narratives. I cherish the warm reception I received in each of these places.

During some down time, I went back to the zoo.

I stopped and prayed at the monument to those arrested on Kristallnacht that stands by the stream. Then I hoped to find some wolves. After searching in vain for over an hour, I did the next best thing. I bought a small hand-painted *Schleich* wolf figurine in the gift shop.

It will remind me how much better things are for Jews in Leipzig today than in 1938 and 1982.

My Leipzig wolf will also remind me – as I hope one day it will remind my children and my grandchildren – that it is our job to make the future better still.

Chapter 4

Vickie's Perspective

In addition to my work in synagogues and churches, a major component of our trips to Germany was the teaching my wife, Vickie, and I did in German High Schools.

Pastor Ursula Sieg and Mr. Wolfgang Henke created an exhibit based on the life journey of Vickie's 97-year-old Mother, Stefanie Steinberg, from Breslau to Barcelona, to Switzerland to New York, to Los Angeles and eventually to San Francisco. The exhibit is the springboard from which Vickie and I taught hundreds of German high school students about the Shoah. The essays that follow reflect her sensitive observations and insightful perspectives on our journeys to Germany.

Confronting My Fear of Kraków

Like so many other baby boomers' parents, mine did not speak to me, when I was a child, of their experiences during World War II. They both had slight German accents. I knew they had left Germany because of Hitler, and I saw the numbers on the arms of so many of their friends. I knew something bad had happened to them and to their friends, these kind and gentle people, who treated me as if I were someone special, a precious life.

As a teenager, I read books that had been published recently, and began to learn of the horrors my parents' friends had lived through and somehow survived. I asked my parents questions, but the answers they gave were limited, as though they were trying to protect me from knowledge that could somehow hurt me. For a high school paper, I interviewed two of my parents' close friends, and though they told of starvation, and forced marches through the snow, I felt that they too were trying to protect me. Or perhaps much was too painful for them to call to mind.

Then I read *Night*, by Elie Wiesel, and I was no longer protected from the facts. I read *Elli*, by Livia Bitton Jackson, which was so painful to read that I couldn't begin to imagine how she had the strength to survive. But she did. I read about the fact that some Jews who survived the camps returned to their home cities and towns, only to be shot and killed by the people who had taken their homes and didn't want to give them back. I knew that Kraków was one of those places.

Kraków is near Auschwitz. Steve and I went there, but I was almost afraid to go. We walked through what had once been the Jewish section of town, and saw three synagogues. One dated back to the 1500s and is now a museum. Another, nearly as old, is in use, and the day we were there people were praying inside because it was the holiday of *Simchat Torah*, the day Jews rejoice in reading the very end of the fifth book of the Torah, Deuteronomy, and immediately begin reading the beginning of the first book of the Torah, Genesis. I sat in the women's section, because it was an Orthodox synagogue. A group of Israeli high school girls sat there too. That was truly a joy to see. The third synagogue was newer, built as a Reform synagogue. Another group of Israeli students was waiting to go inside there.

Yet my heart was still aching for the 3,000,000 Polish Jews who perished in the Holocaust. And our next stop was Auschwitz.

As we drove through the picturesque countryside, I thought of those Jewish people from Kraków, and all over Europe, who had ridden in trains with no windows, no doors, no seats, and no toilets, for whom this trip had been their last.

We took a wrong turn, and went to Birkenau first, one and a half kilometers from the main entrance to Auschwitz. I was wearing socks and shoes, exercise pants under my slacks, and three layers of clothing under my coat. It was windy, and I was cold. I thought of the forced marches, and my parents' friends marching barefoot with only thin layers of clothing.

How cold they must have been.

Thankfully, there were few people at Birkenau when we were there. I was struck by the vastness of the place. Most of the buildings were gone, so one really could see how enormous the place was. We went solemnly into a couple of buildings, and, scanning the horizon, could see some of the chimneys where the ovens had been. The death factory. I silently said Kaddish.

We got back into the car and found the entrance to Auschwitz. We parked in a lot across the street, but I was not prepared for the parking lot near the entrance.

It was 9:00 a.m. and I counted twelve huge tour buses twelve medium-sized buses, and several taxis. Hundreds of people were milling around waiting to get in. I got in line to get entrance tickets, told the lady that we did not need a guide, and to my surprise, was told that the tickets were free. After a long security line, we were inside, and walked to the infamous sign that says "Arbeit macht frei." I shuddered. Here I was surrounded by people, and heard Japanese, French, English, Spanish, German, Polish, and other languages I didn't recognize. Some of the barracks had been made into museums which told about what had happened there. There were so many people in every room listening to their guides that I could barely pass through.

While I could have easily spent an entire day there, we did not have the time, and left to drive to the city of my mother's birth, in what was once Breslau, Germany, but is now Wrocław, Poland.

Yes, I was nervous about going to Kraków and Auschwitz, but I am glad that I went.

A Weekend of Opposites, or Was It?

Friday morning began in Berlin, Germany, at 7:00 a.m. Stephen and I met with a young American, a son of rabbis, who is now living and working in Berlin. At 8:30 Steve led morning worship at Geiger College with young rabbinical and cantorial students thirsty for the knowledge he was imparting, and eager for connections with other Jewish people. I love meeting with these students and learning about their personal histories and why they have chosen to become Jewish leaders in Europe. After a while I left to go walking and shopping, while Stephen then conducted a three-hour seminar.

The pastoral scenery on our afternoon train ride to Leipzig helped soothe our always-emotional entry into that historic city.

We were greeted on the railroad platform by a wonderful German Lutheran pastor, Timotheus Arndt, who has for each of our recent visits to Leipzig eased our way into the city. He drove us to our destination as guests of the wonderful Pfarrerin (clergy) of the Thomaskirche, and then picked us up again at 6:30 to bring us to a Lutheran church social hall, where Angela Langford-Stefan, the Pastorin at that church, had organized a Shabbat dinner for us.

Outreach and making connections are among the clergy's goals, so whereas in some parts of Germany Catholics and Lutherans go their separate ways, members of the Catholic community were invited to participate in this dinner. Stephen spoke about many aspects of Shabbat and explained the week's Torah portion. Then we lit candles, sang the kiddush, and ate a most delicious challah. Dinner was pot luck, and people brought delicious vegetarian delicacies that they had made.

One particular dish was made with grated carrots,

raisins, apples, and almonds. I commented at the end that that dish reminded me of one my mother used to make when I was a child. As we were leaving, a man who had been grumping around previously, and had smiled for no one, walked up to me, puffed out his chest, and said "I made that salad." Full of smiles, he proceeded to tell me, in German, exactly how he had made it.

Saturday morning we went to Services at the Orthodox shul, where we were welcomed warmly, and treated to a wonderful meal in the sukkah after Services. I was thrilled to see that there were quite a number of young families there, in fact two families brought infants. The large sukkah was full of people talking, laughing, and eating. My heart was full of joy to see and be a part of this!

Next stop: The Thomaskirche (where J.S. Bach had been organist and choirmaster). Originally it had been a Catholic Church, but after the Reformation it had become a Lutheran church. There we attended a Motet Service, with music provided by members of the magnificent Gevanthouse Orchestra of Leipzig, the boys choir, the adult choir, and several soloists whose voices were incredible. The church seats 1,800 people. Every seat was full, and the standing-room areas were also filled to the brim. When the 2,000 voices of the congregation sang full throttle with the choir and the organ, the sound was really something to hear.

After the Motet, Pastor Robert Moore and his lovely wife, Kathy, invited us for coffee and cake. Coffee and cake in late afternoon is a German custom that I really enjoy. Robert and Kathy are from the US, but are living in Leipzig for the next several years, educating groups of people who come from English-speaking countries about Lutheran life in Leipzig and the surrounding areas.

Later, in the brisk evening air, we walked with the fabulous Pfarrarin of the Thomaskirche, Britta Taddiken, until we found a restaurant that had room for the three of us. We'd been turned away at four others, all packed to the

Rabbi Fuchs delivers the sermon at Thomaskirche.

gills (note to self, make reservations in advance next time!) until we found one at last, and the food was quite delicious.

After dinner, Pfarrarin Taddiken took us on a walking tour of the city, and as we toured the campus of the University of Leipzig, I realized that my grandmother must have walked these same streets one hundred years ago when she was a student at this university.

On Sunday evening at the 6:00 p.m. Service at the Thomaskirche, Stephen had the honor of delivering the sermon. Unlike the sermon he had given there on Kristallnacht two years ago, in German (for which he practiced the entire day before under the tutelage of Pastorin Ursula Sieg), he planned to give this one in English. The text had been written out and translated into German by Ursula Sieg, to be distributed as a handout to the congregants so they could follow along as he spoke if they needed to.

But...

Although we went to sleep at a relatively normal hour Saturday night, neither Stephen nor I could sleep. In the parsonage, we had separate small bedrooms, and when I couldn't sleep, I decided to read quietly in the living room. When I got there at about 3:00 a.m., I noticed a light under the closed door in his room, so I knocked. He looked at me with his huge beautiful blue eyes, and said, "You won't believe this. I just received this email. You have to read it!" So I sat down on his bed and read.

Soon tears were filling my eyes. This is amazing, I agreed.

The letter was from a young man, also originally from New Jersey, who was living in Leipzig with his wife and son. He and his wife had met at University in England more than twenty years before. That night, he was googling his own name to see if there were any news reports about any of his upcoming art shows.

His name? Stephen Lewis!

He came upon an article by Rabbi Stephen Lewis Fuchs, in which Steve had written about the trip he had made to Leipzig to see the city of his father's birth, and how he had gone to the river by the zoo, because that is where, he had read, they had taken the Jews on Kristallnacht, November 9, 1938. That night the German government had destroyed beautiful, historic synagogues all over Germany, and looted and destroyed Jewish stores. Stephen Lewis Fuchs wanted to see where they took his father. It was a very emotional trip for him, and his writings about that trip were emotional as well.

The young man, Stephen Lewis, became very emotional when he read the account, late Saturday night.

You see, when he first moved to Leipzig, he had lived in an apartment below an elderly couple with whom he had made friends, and for whom he had carried groceries and done small jobs that would have been difficult for them. They became close, and one evening when the wife had gone out, the old man began telling Stephen, the young artist, about an event many years before.

He told him of his best friend growing up, and how he and his Jewish friend were inseparable and did so many things together. With tears in his eyes, and visibly shaking, the old man told Stephen about the night that the Jews were rounded up and taken to the stream by the zoo. He went there and was standing in the street in utter disbelief. When he saw a Nazi soldier peeing down on the Jews, he yelled and said, "How can you do that, are you crazy? These are human beings," at which point he was struck and knocked to the ground. Then what did he see but his best friend, down there, standing in the stream. They locked eyes. And he could do nothing to help him.

For so many years this now-old man had held on to his grief, his shame, and his guilt. But he told the story to the young artist, Stephen.

Stephen Lewis read about Rabbi Stephen Lewis Fuchs' father after midnight, on the one weekend that we were in Leipzig, in the wee hours of the morning of the day that Rabbi Stephen Lewis Fuchs was to speak at the famous church.

Rabbi Stephen wrote back immediately and invited Stephen to attend the service. The artist wrote back that he wouldn't miss it for anything. We all had chills. Rabbi Stephen reconstructed his speech to include this in his talk. Those who could not understand the English read the prepared sermon in German.

Those who could understand were also amazed and touched.

At this service were new friends, as well as friends we had made last year. Stephen invited the new and old friends to join us for a dinner in a nearby restaurant and that brought the weekend to a close.

It was quite a weekend. One I shall always treasure, and never forget.

A Newfound Compassion

While I have always felt that I am a very compassionate and empathetic person, one group of people for whom I have never felt compassion are the Germans of World War II. They murdered 6,000,000 Jewish people, one and a half MILLION of whom were CHILDREN!!! They maimed millions more, both physically and emotionally. They murdered countless others who in their eyes were not good examples of the Aryan image which Hitler wanted to have as the only people in Germany.

Every time I set foot in Germany, I shudder. When I was first there in 1967 it was only 22 years after World War II was over. The soldiers who were in their 20s in the 1940s, were now in their 40s, and in the primes of their lives. I looked around in every city, and said to myself, how many Jews did that man kill, or that man, or that woman. I spent that summer with friends of my father who were not Jewish but had known his family before the war. They showed me the house where my father grew up. I wanted to get out of the car and knock on the door but they wouldn't let me. They showed me the synagogue my father attended as a boy, which for some reason had not been destroyed, but which no one now, was allowed to enter. They were kind to me and took me to different parts of Germany. Then the mother told me that the Americans had bombed their city because of the Krupp factory. She was unhappy that some of her crystal had been cracked. I just stood and stared at her, at 18 years old I didn't know how to respectfully tell her that that was a small price to pay for her people having killed 6,000,000 of mine.

When we were there briefly in 1982, I looked at the men who were now in their 60s and I asked myself which one of these killed the people in my mother's hometown, my father's hometown, my husband's father's hometown. Why said in my heart, "Why do you have the right to walk these streets unafraid when you instilled fear in so many?" I stuck out my pregnant belly and said, "Well, you didn't get my parents, and you're not getting my children."

When Steve and I went back to Germany in 2014 to work with high school students, and just Steve in churches and seminaries, the "brown shirts" were old. My parents' age. I still shudder every time I see a man in Germany of that age. I still ask myself, what did he do, was he a Nazi?

The high school students that we are privileged to teach In Germany are open-minded and speak very good English. They know their grandparents did something, but they don't know what, because no one talks about it. It is as if nothing happened. But these young people know something happened. They are open to hear what we say.

When I ask these students why they think that riding trains in Germany still gives me the creeps, they stare at me, not knowing what to say. When I tell them, I assume that when they ride the trains, they don't think about the seats, or the doors, or the bathrooms, or the windows. They nod their heads in agreement. Then I tell them that when I sit on a train, I am grateful for these things, because the trains my relatives of my parents' generation had no door, window, chair, or toilet when they were forced to enter and ride to their deaths in the camps. I tell them that I look out the windows and wonder if the forests outside are thick enough for people to hide in, so they won't be shot, and I see how close the houses are to the train tracks and I know that the people knew. I know that they knew, and most didn't do anything to help.

Our talks are enhanced by an exhibit with photos of my mother, her parents, and their lives. The exhibit was made possible by Pastor Ursula Sieg and high school (Gymnasium) teacher Wolfgang Henke. I am impressed by the students' compassion. After one such 90-minute session, with 150 students sitting around us on chairs and tables, a group of students circled me, and another circled Steve. And one boy asked me, "How are we supposed to go to our regular classes (as if nothing happened) after this?" This group of students as well as other groups said that they had read things in books, but that we had humanized it, we had made it real for them. They saw for the first time that Jews were just like them, like any other people. They were so moved by the presentation that they had to process what they had heard and discussed before they could return to their normal day. And they wanted to hug us, as if we had become family.

I felt compassion for those students. Wait, but they were German. Yes. And they had nothing to do with the killing of the 6,000,000 and they were as horrified as we that it happened.

The next year, we brought the exhibit to several churches. People came up to me after services and poured their hearts out. I was stunned.

One woman, about 85 had witnessed something horrific happening to a five-year-old Jewish boy. She was five-years-old at the time. She was helpless to save him, but she saw. And she told me over and over, "I saw, I saw." No one can say that these things didn't happen. And she went on and on. And I realized she had never been allowed to speak of it. This exhibition gave her permission to speak of it. I felt compassion for her. Another German. But she had been so small, and the killings were not her doing.

Another person that same day came to me and told me that her father used to sing and play the guitar before the war. When he came home he only sat on the couch depressed. No more singing, nothing. But he didn't speak of it either so she didn't know what happened. Our exhibit and talk at least gave her some insight, and freedom to speak. I felt compassion for her too. And even for her father. Who knows what he saw, and felt powerless to prevent, and guilty for, for the rest of his life.

In the tiny town of Sultzberg where Steve led Yom Kippur services, I met a lady whose mother left her husband when he became a Nazi and wouldn't let her child go to the school where she would have been indoctrinated into Nazi thought. What a brave lady! This woman (who had been the child) took it upon herself to map where all the Jews in this small town had lived, where their shops had been, who was killed and who escaped. She showed us the door posts of houses which were indented where mezuzot had once been. For her, I felt compassion and respect.

For the Nazis as a whole, I will never feel any compassion. But for my generation of Germans and the ones after, some compassion is inching its way into my heart. Nazis are their parents and grandparents, but they are not. They are still learning about what happened, and I always recommend that the read the book *Night* by Elie Wiesel, so that they will know what really happened, and they too will feel compassion for those killed and permanently injured.

Compassion.

The high school students that we teach are helping me feel some compassion for Germans. At least for the generation of today's high school students who take our teaching into their hearts. They cannot undo what the Nazis did. But they can work to prevent it from happening again. And I believe in my heart that many of them will.

From Breslau to Neumünster

From Breslau to Neumünster is not so far, but it is a longer journey if the route is via, Spain, Switzerland, New York, Los Angeles and San Francisco. But that is the route my mother-in-law, Stefanie Steinberg, now 93-years young, has taken.

Stefanie was born in Breslau and spent a happy childhood there displaying remarkable talent as an artist. But when the storm clouds of Nazi hegemony threatened the idyllic existence – indeed childhood itself – ended for her

In her own words:

My father realized that Germany was becoming a dangerous place, and suddenly the government no longer permitted him to treat Kranken Kasse patients, his primary group of patients. He began to make preparations to take us out of Germany. During that time, he was again given the permit to treat the workers because he had been a decorated officer in World War I, and had been given the Iron Cross.

Wisely, he had the foresight to take his family out in 1936. He brought us to Barcelona, Spain, where he set up a medical practice, having brought his radiology equipment with him. Six months later, the Spanish Civil War broke out, and the women and children of foreigners were forced to evacuate the country. Father could not leave until much later and had no possibility to work in Switzerland. My mother, brother, and I had small bags packed, and we went by refugee boat to Marseille, and from there by train to Zurich, Switzerland. With the help of Julius Schueller and the International Council of Jewish Women, I was sent to Kinderheim, Wartheim, in Heiden, Canton Appenzell as an unpaid helper, a Practicantin with two other teenage girls and about forty children. My mother went to Dijon, France, to work as a secretary for a woman professor, and my brother was sent to live with a family in Switzerland who treated him poorly. Much later, my father went to New York to try to set up a medical practice there.

When I first arrived at the Heim, I was quite shell-shocked, and the other people there called me the Steffie who does not talk. After a while, I began to thrive, and even taught the children a calisthenics class outside. After I had been there about a year, the children put on a play for the delegates of the Council of Jewish Women, and I painted the whole backdrop, a forest scene. When the delegates saw what I had painted, they helped me to get a scholarship to attend an art school, called the Kunst-schule Muench-Winkel in Zurich. I was able to attend that school for about a year, until 1938.

In the summer of 1938, my mother and I boarded a boat in Le Havre, bound for New York. My brother could not leave Switzerland until he graduated from the Institute Juventus in Zurich. He came in October of 1938, just a few weeks before Kristallnacht. When we boarded the boat, I had just had my 17th birthday. It so happened that I met my future husband, Ulrich Steinberg, whom I would marry seven years later, on the boat.

Unfortunately, when we arrived in New York, I didn't attend high school; I went straight to work. One of my first jobs in New York was in a lady's hat shop on Diekman Street, sewing felt onto hats. For that, I was paid $5.00 a week, far less than someone who was born in the US would have been paid. Sometimes I had to work until 10:00 at night, and Uli would pick me up from work and bring me home half asleep, using the subway.

My next job was at a store called Jane Engel, on Madison Avenue, an elegant store not far from where we lived, where I was paid $7.00 a week. I worked there for about three years. I would usually walk home for the lunch my father prepared for me. His doctor's office was then on the ground floor, and *we lived on the third floor above his office. Later, I worked painting on ceramics and on silk ties. When my father became sick with cancer, I worked in the mornings, and in the afternoon I visited my father in the hospital. My brother took mornings off in order to visit him. When my father died, at Mount Zion Hospital, where he had volunteered in the outpatient department, the hospital would not release his body because my brother and I did not have enough money to pay the fee. Eventually they released him, and my brother and I moved into his small office and living quarters.*

I decided to leave New York and worked my way to California, where I looked up Uli in the phonebook. We married a few months later, in April of 1945, and lived in his tiny bachelor apartment.

For a while, I painted on silk ties, and then I painted a blouse for myself. I wore it to the Ambassador Hotel gift shop on Wilshire Boulevard in Los Angeles, and asked the owners to give me some of the blouses, called "dogs" that they could not sell. I painted them, and they sold like "hot cakes". I painted more and more blouses, and even painted a ball gown for the actress Joan Fontaine to wear in the movie, "Emperor Waltz" (about Franz Joseph) which she starred in with Bing Crosby. The famous movie designer, Edith Head, had asked me to paint the ball gown. We then rented the top floor of an office building, and hired 10 artists to paint my designs. We sold our creations all over the US. We painted on blouses, ties, bras, girdles, swim suits, undergarments. It became a big company. At that time, I also took classes at the Art Center School. Then a large Chicago company brazenly copied our bestselling flamingo blouses. After the lawsuits, money ran low, our company folded, and I worked as a designer for a factory that made decorated clothes. Shortly after that, we moved to San Francisco, and began anew.

In San Francisco, I had the chance to take classes at San Francisco State University, which was in walking distance from our apartment. I took classes in drawing, painting, and art history. I became a member of a long established organization called The San Francisco Women Artists, served on its board for many years, had many paintings and photographs exhibited in their gallery over the years, and became its president for two years as well. I am still a senior member, after more than 50 years, and they chose to feature a painting of mine in one of their most recent exhibitions.

My works were also exhibited in various San Francisco museums, both painting and photography, and while an active member of the Bay Area Photographers, I received numerous awards for photo montages in black and while photography.

In 1989, I joined CLIR, the Center for Learning in Retirement which is part of the University of California. This gave me the chance to attend excellent classes taught by University of California professors, in art, photography, and in how to use the computer to enhance the quality of photographs. I still attend lectures and events there which are intellectually stimulating both because of the high caliber of the lectures, and because of the quality of the other seniors attending, who have become friends over the years.

In my free time I still enjoy painting and taking photographs of subjects which capture my attention. I enjoy visits from my two daughters and sons-in-law, my grandchildren and my great grandchildren. I also take care of my cat, Blackberry, and my garden both in front and in back of my house which I consider to be my personal, private paradise!

Today (October 28) in Neumünster, a wonderful exhibition of Stefanie's life journey ones for edification of high school students. Pastorin Ursula Sieg, with the enthusiastic cooperation of my wife, Vickie, and Stefanie herself, has put together this wonderful interactive learning opportunity. Vickie and I have already met with groups of students doing projects that center around the exhibition. As I write, Vickie is putting the finishing touches on her exhibit-opening speech, and soon we will drive to Neumünster for the event.

At home in San Francisco, Stefanie still is an active artist who lives independently. In a very real way, she has come back home to Germany triumphant over the forces of evil that inflicted years of pain and hardship on her and so many. It is a source of pride to her and all of us who love her that her life journey will teach valuable lessons to a new generation of Germans.

Vickie Fuchs speaks in Wroclaw.

Chapter 5

Kiel

Rita and Horst

After a wonderful study session about Jacob at the Christus Kirche in Bordesholm last night, Vickie and I arrived quite late and very tired in Husum. We are the guests of a most wonderful couple, Rita and Horst Blunk.

Last year they drove an hour each way to Kiel to attend services and study sessions that I led. Before we left to return to the USA, Horst presented me with a clock with Hebrew letters marking the hours that he had made. It has a proud place in my study at home.

When we returned to Germany this year, we learned that Horst and Rita had arranged for me to conduct, tonight, the first Jewish service in the synagogue in Friedrichstadt since the end of World War II.

Earlier today, Vickie and I addressed some three hundred students in an assembly of Senior HS students at the Theodor-Storm Schule in Husum, which Horst had also arranged. For many of them it was the first time they had heard from a rabbi or individuals whose family members were directly affected by the horror of Nazi time.

Rita was born Jewish, but her family did not practice. By profession she is a nurse, but she moves around the kitchen with such grace and alacrity that she could have been a dancer. "The pace in the hospital, is so quick," she said, "that I have to move fast."

Horst officially entered the mikvah and took on the Covenant of the Jewish people one year ago, but his Jewish journey began more than four decades earlier.

As a Christian pastor he began to explore the Jewish roots of his faith by driving 300 kilometers on a regular basis to the synagogue in Hannover. Horst's growing love of Judaism helped Rita reclaim her spiritual identity. Today

Jewish books, artwork and symbols adorn the walls of their lovely house.

On Shabbat morning Rita, Horst, Vickie, and a few others will join for Torah study in their home. I know that, as they always do, Horst and Rita will make interesting observations and raise challenging questions.

I look forward to this Shabbat with great joy!

Return to Friedrichstadt

With great excitement, we return to the northern German city of Friedrichstadt. Last year I had the privilege of conducting the first Jewish service in that city since 1938, a fact verified by the head of the Jewish Cultural Center there, Frau Christiane Thomsen and several others.

Since then, to my joy there have been several Jewish cultural events in that city including the Bat Mitzvah ceremony of Laura Wendt a young woman from Denmark, in a service led by my colleague, Rabiner Dr. Walter Rothschild.

Much credit for the "heavy lifting" in Friedrichstadt as far as replanting Jewish life goes belongs to Horst (Ephraim) and Rita (Devorah) Blunk.

I had the privilege of making their acquaintance for the first time in 2014 during adult education sessions and services that I conducted with Walter Joshua Pannbacker in Kiel, a full hour away from their home. The desire of Horst and Rita – and the activity that inspires that desire – to revitalize Jewish life in their home region inspire me.

Without question the experience last year of conducting the first Jewish service there since Kristallnacht was a great thrill. It was even more gratifying to lead prayer in the Friedrichstadt synagogue because it had been commandeered and turned into a headquarters for Nazi officers after November 9, 1938.

The experience reminded me of a recollection shared in a talk to us students by the then Dean of the California branch of the Hebrew Union College-Jewish Institute of Religion by the late Rabbi Dr. Alfred Gottschalk (who went on to become President of the entire four-campus College-Institute). Gottschalk recalled a trip he took to Rome and his feeling as he stood beneath the famous Arch of Titus. In the arch is an inscription from the year 70 C.E., "Judaea capta." Judaea is captured, and by implication, Judaism is no more. Gottschalk related how he looked up with pride at that inscription, and proclaimed, "Here I am Titus! Where are you and your empire now?"

During our worship in Friedrichstadt last year, I remembered Gottschalk's words, and I said to myself, "Here we are, Hitler. Where are you and your empire now?"

Because of all the Jewish cultural activity that takes place in Friedrichstadt now, this year's service will not have the same novel, first-time-since-Kristallnacht feeling that last year's did.

And that is a good thing!

My goal is not to be the first in a generation to represent Jewish life in different places in Germany. My goal is for Progressive Jewish life to become a regular, vibrant and contributing part of German culture once again. My second opportunity to lead worship in Friedrichstadt feels like a small but meaningful step toward that precious goal.

A Ray of Light that Pierced the Darkness

Memorial at the site of the Great Synagogue of Kiel, Germany, that was destroyed on Kristallnacht, November 9-10, 1938. I will speak at the Kiel Kristallnacht commemorative, sponsored by The Organization for Christians and Jews Working Together, the evening of November 9, 2016.

Tomorrow, is the anniversary of *Kristallnacht*, known to Germans as *Pogromnacht*, the nationwide pogrom perpetrated by the Nazis against Germany's Jews on November 9-10, 1938. Historians consider this event the formal beginning of the Holocaust.

As we commemorate this somber anniversary, I want to share an act of heroism by a German citizen, a ray of light that momentarily pierced the darkness of Nazi terror.

Rabbi Lawrence Kushner recounts:

A Jewish woman was riding home from work on a city bus when storm troopers boarded the coach to examine the identification papers of the passengers. The SS men ordered all of those with Jewish papers to leave the bus and get on a big truck waiting nearby.

As the soldiers made their way through the bus, a Jewish woman began to sob softly. When the Gentile man next to her asked her what was wrong, she answered that she was Jewish, and the soldiers would surely take her.

All of a sudden, the man shouted at her, "You stupid wretch! I can't stand being near you!" The SS men asked the man what all the shouting was about.

He pointed to the woman and sneered, "My dumb wife

has forgotten her papers again. She does this all the time. I'm fed up with her."

The SS men laughed, shook their heads, and moved on.

The woman never learned the name of the German stranger who had saved her life.

Chapter 6

Pastors' Convention

Why We Should Thank Eve for Our Lives of Meaning

It was with some trepidation that I arrived at the regional Lutheran Pastors' convention in the quaint German town of Preetz. I had been invited by Pastor Anke Wolff-Steger to keynote the convention with a sermon on the Garden of Eden. Because Pastor Wolff-Steger had invited me to speak on this topic at her church a year ago, she knew the gist of what I would say. The pastors in attendance did not, and I knew some would be taken aback.

I quickly reviewed the classical Christian interpretation (surely, they did not need me for that) that Eden marked the "Fall of Man." We had everything we could possibly want in the garden, but Eve ruined everything by eating of the Tree of Knowledge, the one tree from which God warned the first couple not to eat and then convincing Adam to eat as well. In so doing, they plunged humanity into a state of sinfulness, but belief in the saving power of Jesus' life, death on the cross, ascension to heaven, and resurrection saves us from that degraded state.

It was a surprise to no one there, of course, when I said that Jews do not believe that interpretation. For traditional Jews, eating from the Tree of Knowledge was a profound act of disobedience, and we live with the consequences, a life of limited duration, pain in childbirth, and the need to work for a living. But we do not exist in a state of sinfulness, and therefore we have no need for Jesus to save us.

Then I shared a perspective on Eden that is included in my book, *What's in It for Me? Finding Ourselves in Biblical Narratives*, the essence of which I first learned from a beloved Bible professor at Hebrew Union College-Jewish Institute of Religion, Chanan Brichto, of blessed memory:

Eden was a nice place to visit but not to live. It was a

world of no birth, no death, and no sexuality. Indeed, sexual knowledge is precisely the knowledge the first couple discovered when they ate of the Tree of Knowledge.

Eve is not the villain of the story but the heroine. She is not interested in an endless life of ease without challenge or purpose. Although she did not know what life outside the garden would be like, she was willing to risk that uncertainty for a life filled with meaningful achievement, satisfying relationships, and the ability to bring new life into the world.

I can relate. After a long year of work, I would love to visit Eden, a place where all my needs are provided, and I can lie on a pristine beach with fresh ripe fruit hanging over my head.

I would love it for about a week, maybe even 10 days. After that I would seek out a challenge that would bring meaning to my life.

That is how I imagine Eve felt when she chose to eat the fruit. We should see Eve as a hero whose bold action enables us all to live lives of meaning and purpose.

However differently we interpret the story of Eden, I concluded, we can agree on one thing. None of us lives there anymore. We all live in this imperfect world. Therefore, God calls on each of us to work as best we can to make the world a better place.

After breakfast, we spent an hour studying the texts in small *chevruta* (literally, "fellowship," but in this instance, text study groups that generally comprise pairs of students). I truly believe studying Torah or Bible together is one of the most productive and honest ways to experience inter-religious dialogue. As we studied one of the pastors challenged me: "How can you call Eve a hero when she defied a direct command from God."

I responded that rather than a command, I see an admonition in the text that there would be consequences for eating from the tree, and that Eve was willing to take the risk. I added that I don't believe this is the only reasonable interpretation of the story, but I think it is reasonable for you to give it some thought. Sometimes when we first hear an idea it jars us but begins to make more sense over time.

Her response was a quizzical look, but as I left the gathering, I noticed that she had purchased my book and had begun to look through it. I could not ask for more.

Pastors' Convention in Breklum

So ...

Here I am at the Christian Jensen Kolleg in Breklum, Germany.

What am I doing here?

I am invited to address a regional convention for Lutheran Pastors on the concept of "Memory" in Jewish Thought and to connect those ideas to a Jewish Theology after Auschwitz.

Wow! Am I nervous!

All the anxieties and fears and nervous feelings that well up in me any time I speak to any group anywhere are multiplied to the fourth power.

To make me even more nervous, the Propst (Area-wide Supervising Pastor) Stefan Block, who invited me, let me know that as far as the conference attendees are concerned, "You are a surprise visitor." That means these Pastors are unaware that a Rabbi will address them tonight.

Yikes! What if...

...they do not want to hear a Rabbi?

...my talk stinks?

...they laugh at me?

Now, a good part of me knows I am overplaying my fears. But the fear is real nonetheless.

My room at the College is lovely – spacious and airy with lots of green trees in full bloom right outside my window.

Now I have just returned from lunch.

It was a welcome relief to be greeted so warmly by two wonderful Pastors at whose churches I have spoken in past years: Martina Dittkrist from Kaltenkirchen and

Anke Wolff-Steger from Schulensee. I have such wonderful memories of how each of these Pastors welcomed Vickie and me to their communities and hosted us after the service for a delicious lunch in their homes.

Seeing them and feeling the genuine warmth of their smiles has made me feel more comfortable. I am still nervous, but I feel a bit more at-ease now.

The Next Morning

I am feeling gratified. The presentation went very well in large measure because I spent the afternoon listening, listening, and listening to their own struggles and the struggles of their families and parishioners with the memories of what they were doing during the Hitler years.

Hearing their struggles somehow took the jumble of material swirling around in my head and helped it come out in a coherent one-hour presentation that I offered without notes of any kind.

After a fifteen-minute break there were probing questions and, I pray, helpful answers. I left them with the thought that their questions were more important than my answers. I stressed the importance of memory as a lesson from which to learn.

And I emphasized as I do before almost every German audience I address:

Wir können die Vergangenheit nicht ungeschehen machen, aber wir können gemeinsam an einer besseren Zukunft arbeiten!

We cannot undo the past, but we can work together to shape a better future ...

...for our children, grandchildren and all the generations that will follow.

Chapter 7

Family and Friends

Yahrzeit in Edinburgh

On Sunday, January 31, I had the privilege of being (I was told) the first rabbi to deliver a sermon at the historic St. Giles Cathedral, the Mother Church of Scotland.

I consider it more than a coincidence that event took place on the 45th anniversary of my father's death.

The connection is particularly stark because my sermon was part of an interfaith Holocaust Memorial Service, and my father was a survivor.

He was arrested on Kristallnacht, November 9, 1938, and taken to Dachau where the Nazis shaved his head and beat him. But he was so very fortunate because seven out of every nine Jews who lived in his native city of Leipzig in 1935 died in the Shoah.

Because my father's relatives in the United States had the necessary papers in order, they were able to secure his release after only a few weeks. He came to this country, met and happily married a beautiful American woman, and fathered my sister and me.

Yes, he was so fortunate to escape, but I know the residual effects of his suffering contributed to his death at age 57 while his two older brothers – who left Germany earlier – lived well into their eighties.

When the Beadle of the Cathedral formally summoned me to ascend the St. Giles pulpit, my mind flashed back 45 years to when I received that horrible call from my mother while I was studying in Jerusalem.

Back then an international phone call was a very big deal. If you got one, it was your birthday, some other special occasion, or something was very wrong.

When my landlady, Mrs. Daniel Auster, widow of the

Rabbi Fuchs on the St. Giles pulpit.

former Mayor of Jerusalem came into my room at 5:00 a.m. to tell me my mother was on the phone, I knew it could only be one thing. My precious father, in my mother's words, "was gone."

The long plane ride home – which stopped in Paris was excruciating. Sitting next to me on the first leg of the flight was an ebullient woman on her way to Paris to celebrate her daughter's wedding.

I did not have the heart to deflate her joy by sharing the reason I was on the plane. My stomach was in knots as I listened to her.

I spent thirty days at home before returning to Jerusalem to continue my studies. They were precious days of reflection and remembrance.

They confirmed for me the wisdom of our tradition in advising us to take sufficient time to absorb the blow when a loved one dies.

I loved my father and admired him, but there are so many questions I would have liked to ask that I never did.

Why didn't you leave Germany earlier? What was it like when you first came to the USA?

You always acted like you loved me, but why did you never tell me?

In the days following my second open-heart surgery in 2012, I found myself depressed and concerned for my future. I sought therapy and was not surprised when the doctor zeroed in on my relationship with my dad.

"You seem to have never been able to please him," he noted.

I credit the Eternal One and the therapist for the blessings I have enjoyed since my surgery: the three months I spent as rabbi in Milan, Ben's marriage to Kristin, the birth of our fifth grandchild, Flora, the completion of my book, its translation into German, the two extended periods Vickie and I spent in Germany, the many places I have been privileged to speak, and of course, our recent trip to Scotland.

Indeed, the future about which I fretted at the time of my surgery has turned out very nicely.

I believe in the things I am doing and hope they make a small difference for good.

But I know the doctor was correct. I still want to please my father. And maybe, just maybe, I am beginning to believe I am.

The Parsonage Has a Sukkah!

The Jewish harvest festival of Sukkot begins tonight, five days after Yom Kippur. We celebrate by building a *sukkah*, a small hut outside our homes to symbolize the temporary homes of our ancestors while they traveled through the desert after being freed from slavery in Egypt.

"A child who has the experience of building a sukkah," my Theology/Liturgy Professor, Jakob J. Petuchowski, of blessed memory, used to tell us, "has a Jewish experience worth six months of Sunday school."

The outstanding American writer, Noah Gordon, in his 1964 best-selling novel *The Rabbi*, captured the essence of just how important a *sukkah* can be for a child: "The bond between Michael and his *zaydeh (*grandfather*)* grew stronger during the early fall, when the days began to shorten, and the autumn feast of Sukkot drew near. Each autumn during his four-year stay with the Rivkins, *Zaydeh* built in their postage-stamp back yard a *sukkah,* or ceremonial hut. The *sukkah* was a small house of wooden planks covered with boughs and sheaves. It was hard work for an old man to build it, especially since hayfields, corn shocks and trees were not plentiful in Brooklyn. Sometimes he had to go deep into Jersey for raw materials, and he badgered Abe for weeks until he was driven to the country in the family Chevrolet.

'Why do you bother?' Dorothy asked him once when she brought a glass of tea to where he strained and perspired to raise the hut. 'Why do you work so hard?'

'To celebrate the harvest.'

'What harvest, for God's sake? We're not farmers. You

sell canned goods. Your son makes corsets for ladies with big behinds. Who has a harvest?'

He looked pityingly at this female his son had made his daughter.

'For thousands of years, since the Jews emerged from the Wilderness, in ghettos and in palaces they have observed Sukkot. You don't have to raise cabbages to have a harvest.' His big hand grasped Michael behind the neck and pushed him toward his mother. 'Here is your harvest.' She didn't understand, and by then Zaydeh had been living with them long enough not to expect understanding from her."

Our family *sukkah* to which we invited congregants every year was a very precious part of our family's Jewish identity over the years. Our children were fascinated by it as babies, loved decorating it as children, and helped set it up when they were older. They loved inviting their non-Jewish friends over to help decorate. Now they have children of their own and celebrate Sukkot with them.

Each year we looked forward to having our congregants join us for a reception in the *sukkah*. As much as our sukkah meant to our children, it meant at least as much to us.

In addition to the huts our ancestors lived in when they wandered through the desert for 40 years, the *sukkah* today symbolizes that too many have homes to live in all year around that offer no more protection against the elements than these fragile huts. The *sukkah* teaches us that the less fortunate are our responsibility. We cannot in good conscience turn away.

Yes, Rabbi Petuchowski was right about the *sukkah* and six months of Sunday school. In fact, I think he might have understated the case.

In Bad Segeberg, Germany, our hosts Pastorin Ursula Sieg and Pastor Martin Pommerening got wind of how important the custom was to us back home and took it on themselves to erect a sukkah in their backyard.

With Vickie, Pastorin Ursula Sieg and Pastor Martin Pommerening in the sukkah.

This gesture means so much to us. This *sukkah* more than any other we have ever enjoyed symbolizes our hope for inter-religious cooperation and reconciliation that inspired us to spend these ten weeks in Germany.

Eternal God, spread סוכת שלום "the *Sukkah* of Peace" over us, over all Israel and over all humanity! May we may dwell in it together in harmony!

Haedicke

The depth of her kindness, intellect and beauty present themselves gently. There is nothing pretentious about her.

And yet ...

One marvels at how she does so much so efficiently.

Keren-Miriam Foerst Haedicke is first and foremost a devoted single mother of two beautiful and sensitive children. Seeing to their needs is a full-time job.

She is also an Ob-Gyn physician whose busy practice and the enormous number of women who depend on her for care and comfort are far more than a full-time job.

Given all she has on her plate I marvel at how Dr. Foerst Haedicke found the time to plan and attend to every single detail of the wonderful four days Vickie and I spent in Flensburg. She arranged with the local High School for Vickie and me to present three 90-minute lessons about Judaism and the Holocaust to three different classes. She spent considerable time with the coordinating teacher working out the particulars.

She arranged for me to speak at two Kristallnacht commemorations. The first was at the Jewish cemetery and the second (along with Vickie) at the magnificent Church of St. Nikolai. The experiences were unforgettable.

She also set up two very well-attended opportunities for me to speak about my book, *What's in It for Me? Finding Ourselves in Biblical Narratives.* The first was in Roman Catholic church and the second in the synagogue of Flensburg. Both of these events required considerable time and planning.

She also saw to it that we had wonderful tours of major sites in Flensburg and an excursion to villages across the nearby Danish border.

And all of this was on top of her amazing effort to plan, execute and sponsor the Oneg Shabbat for the Kabbalat Shabbat service I conducted which was the first Jewish service held in Friedrichstadt since 1938. How special that was!

On Shabbat morning she and her daughter Hannah joined us and a small group for an extensive look at Chaye Sarah, the weekly Torah portion. Later that evening Vickie, Keren-Miriam and I enjoyed Havdalah together. As we sang for Eliyahu Ha-Navi (Elijah the Prophet) and the hope for the future he represents, we felt like family.

As we left Flensburg and said goodbye to one another all three of us, Vickie, Keren-Miriam and I all hoped that it will not be too long until we share a family reunion.

Ulrike

I never expected she would come to the train station herself ... but there she was. I mean it was one of the biggest days of her life, the day when she was to be formally installed as Pastor of the Ev. Lutheran Church in Brokstedt, Germany.

She wrote that "someone" would meet the train, so we would know how to find the church, but she rode her bike to the station to greet us herself. The four of us walked back to town together, Ulrike, Vickie, the bike and me.

In the hour before the service, a group of young scouts were busily preparing the churchyard for the reception afterwards. They worked with purpose and determination. They seemed so proud to take part in such a special day for the village.

The church was beautiful. Ulrike had asked me to read portions of Psalm 103 in Hebrew while her husband, Pastor Alexander Wolfahrt read the same passages after me in German. It was a touching moment... the choir sang beautifully, and their voices clearly resonated with a feeling of how very special the day was.

Then the Propst, Dr. Kurt Riecke charged Pastor Wolfahrt and the congregation to cherish the bond they had created. Then he invited me up to share a thought with Ulrike and join him in asking God to bless her.

As I walked to the front of the church, my mind flashed back to the first time I met Pastorin Ulrike Wolfahrt in 2015. She was one of the Pastors at the Dietrich Bonhoeffer Church in Neumünster, and she asked me to preach a sermon explaining why Jews do not believe in Jesus as Christians do. She wanted the congregation to hear a frank explanation to the community of this important theological difference between our two religions.

Rabbi Fuchs with Pastorin Ulrike Wohlfahrt.

Her welcome and warm encouragement of me to deal with this difficult subject gave me strength. We formed a bond that day that was very special. We shared a mission to deal with a sensitive subject in a way that was open, honest and mutually respectful.

A year later, on our next visit to Germany she brought her beautiful four-year-old son Samuel to visit me in Bad Segeberg. The three of us took a nice walk on a chilly autumn afternoon and then had cocoa in a lovely coffee shop.

Afterward that visit, Pastor Wolfahrt wrote me that Samuel had said, "I like Stephen because he knows my heart."

And so, as I walked to the front of the church last Sunday, I thought of the biblical passage when Samuel revealed that he chose David to be King over his brothers because God knows his heart (I Samuel 16:7).

And before I placed my hands on her head, to ask God to bless her, I said, "Just as the Biblical Samuel said of David, God has chosen you and Alexander to be parents of your

Samuel and leaders of this church because God knows your heart."

When the Propst formally presented Pastorin Wolfahrt to the congregation, they rose in a touching standing ovation for her. It was a beautiful tribute that sent shivers down my spine.

Then Pastorin Wolfahrt began her sermon about the Prodigal Son (Luke 15: 11-32).

My German is not nearly good enough to understand all that she said, but I know that she spoke with conviction and passion and held the congregation in the palm of her hand.

After the service Pastorin Wolfahrt received the warm congratulations of the many people who crowded the church, and a lovely outdoor picnic reception ensued.

Vickie and I returned to Bad Segeberg filled with joy that we could share such a wonderful event. We felt we had been blessed to witness such an extraordinary moment of spiritual unity between a Pastor and her community.

Days later, the feeling endures.

The Lehrer

In Germany "teacher" (Lehrer) is an honored profession. How refreshing it is to see that!

My wife Vickie taught school for over thirty years. Like too many American educators she was overworked and underpaid. As the years went by, the imperative to "teach to the standardized test" robbed her teaching of much of its creativity and joy.

Here in Germany because of the exhibit about Vickie's mother we have made more than a dozen visits to schools and spoken with more than twenty teachers. Without exception they felt their work was respected, important and appropriately compensated.

The USA could definitely take a lesson from Germany in this regard.

Last year the exhibit stayed in one school, the Holstenschule in Neumünster. For weeks we worked hand in glove with the teacher in charge of the project, Wolfgang Henke. For us Mr. Henke is the epitome of the German teacher. He is modest, soft-spoken, extremely well-schooled and supremely competent. He treats the students with respect and caring, and they treat him the same way.

It is easy to see why.

He spent months preparing for the exhibit with Pastorin Ursula Sieg. Together they set us a Jewish Wohnzimmer (Living Room) in a classroom set aside for that purpose in the Holstenschule last year. Students could come there and chat informally with Vickie and me during certain times when we visited.

This year he spent an additional untold number of hours as a volunteer helping coordinate the visits of the exhibit to several other schools in the area. His dedication is inspiring.

Mr. Henke is also an excellent tennis player, and he graciously invited me to hit with him on an off day at the Tennis Halle in Neumünster.

After five summers as a tennis instructor in a private club in New Jersey and at the famous Concord Hotel in the Catskill mountains, I believe I can tell more about a person's personality by watching him or her for fifteen minutes on the tennis court than I can if I were to interview the individual for half an hour. My observations have nothing to do with how well a person plays but everything to do with his or her demeanor on the court.

In the case of Mr. Henke, all of the qualities I had already observed (and noted above) while working with him were evident when we played. It was a most enjoyable hour that confirmed for me that Wolfgang Henke certainly deserves one of Germany's most honorable titles: *Teacher!*

Rita Goldberg

One of the drawbacks of being in Germany is that I miss important things going on at home at the same time. In 2018, one of those painful "misses" was the funeral of Rita Goldberg. Rita and her husband Dick, who were married more than 50 years – came to Columbia, MD just before I arrived in 1973 as the congregation's "Rabbinic Intern." The congregation had 58 families at the time and grew to 385 during the thirteen years of my tenure there. Much of the credit for the growth goes to the leadership of Dick and Rita over those years. They became fast friends with Vickie and me and were always available for advice for us and for our children at crucial points of their lives. We shared so many times of joy and sadness together.

Dick and Rita were strong supporters of our efforts in Germany. I know Rita would have wanted us to be doing the things we do in Germany rather than be at her funeral. Though my body was far away when she died, my heart was with her and with Dick, and these are the thoughts I sent from Germany that Rabbi Craig Axler graciously read at her funeral.

June 3, 2018

Today, Vickie and I are at the picturesque church in the village of Schulensee in northern Germany where I am preaching to the Lutheran congregation about the events on Mount Sinai and how they can speak meaningfully to Christians as well as to Jews.

Yes, our bodies are in Schulensee but our hearts are at Rita Goldberg's funeral.

From the day I first met her in Columbia, Rita appreciated interfaith outreach, and enthusiastically encouraged my efforts in that realm. I dedicate my words today in her memory.

Growing up in a small town in Pennsylvania with few Jews, Rita particularly appreciated the importance of inter-religious understanding and cooperation. She took a keen interest in what Vickie and I do in Germany, and I dedicate my words today to her memory. Although Rita would be glad we are here, Vickie and I wish we were with Dick and all of you today.

Rita Zieve Goldberg ... I always thought of her as Rita Z.

She was the daughter of a beloved small-town physician who made house calls. Rita inherited his wisdom and compassion.

We met in 1973. They came to Columbia and Temple Isaiah just before I arrived to begin my one-year internship with the congregation. We have been dear friends ever since.

I was first in awe of Rita when I learned she had personally known the great baseball player Richie Allen in high school. The subsequent years would yield more substantive reasons for me to be in awe of Rita.

To me she was ageless. She never seemed young, and – even when we visited her a few weeks back in hospice care – she never seemed old.

Her speech had a unique and endearing lilt, and her laugh was unmistakable. Perhaps it was Rita's greatest triumph that she was able to laugh and smile despite the tragedy and endless list of illnesses that marked her life's path.

The first - of many - volunteer jobs I remember Rita taking on was making peanut butter and jelly sandwiches to serve as a luncheon for the monthly family services Temple Isaiah began holding at Swansfield Neighborhood center.

I remember Dianne Tobin playing a toy organ; I remember the smiling faces of children, some of whom became rabbis, sitting on the floor before me as I told a Shabbat story, but the magic that makes those memories so special was Rita's sandwiches.

Rita wore many hats, loving wife and occasional ego deflator of Dick, devoted mother of Andy, advisor to the rabbi, confidante of Vickie, peerless hostess and dear friend to so many.

As memorable as Rita was as a hostess, she was even more memorable as a guest. When she came to your home for any social occasion, you could count on a beautifully handwritten note of thanks appearing in your mailbox the next business day.

Our lives intersected frequently at events big and small, both joyous and sad. She was a fabulous storyteller.

Her home was a favorite sleepover destination for our son Leo when he was small. Vickie was very pregnant with Sarah when we attended second night Seder at their home in 1979. We always recount how Rita's Matzah balls that evening was the catalyst that sent Vickie into labor to give birth the following day.

Fast-forward to recent days, and it was Rita and Dick who visited our children in San Francisco to give wise council to each of them at a difficult time.

I remember Andy's Bar Mitzvah like it was yesterday. The date was the Shabbat during Sukkot. Because I was very big on having families build Sukkot, I suggested to Andy that his family should build one. It did not take Rita long to appear in my office to share that Sukkah building was not a Goldberg family forte, and that we should think of some other way to connect Andy's Bar Mitzvah to the festival. After we put our heads together, Rita and Andy came up with the idea of a model sukkah made out of Popsicle sticks. I can still see it in my mind.

That episode was so typical of Rita. If sukkah building was not her forte, finding equitable solutions to potential conflicts surely was.

More clearly than the miniature Sukkah, I can still see the joy Rita's face radiated at how much Andy learned and how skillfully he taught the congregation at his Bar Mitzvah.

Inevitably my memories of Rita on that wonderful day in October 1981 scramble discordantly together in my mind with my memories of that horrible day in March of 2009 when Andy died.

There is no greater heartbreak for a mother than to lose a child, and if possible, the heartbreak is even greater when that child is your one and only, and your souls are so inextricably intertwined as are Rita and Dick's souls with Andy's.

And yet Rita pushed on with determination and purpose.

Miraculously she found joy in life despite the horror of losing Andy and despite the incredible list of medical issues with which she lived. Through all she endured, even on her deathbed, Rita was always smiling and always looking for ways to help others.

That is why I will always be genuinely in awe of her.

I cannot say with certainty what happens to Rita now, but my hope is that she is not alone. In my mind's eye I see her reunited with her parents and most of all, with Andy.

She and Dick shared a remarkable marriage of well over 50 years. Truly they were meant for each other, so much so that it is hard to imagine one without the other. No more poignant definition of the word, "Alone," comes to my mind than Dick without Rita.

Together, unfettered by infirmities, they will laugh, smile and revel in each other's company. They will look after one another, and together they will hope that we will look after Dick with the incredible love and devotion with which Dick looked after her.

That is the best way I know to ensure that the memory of Rita Zieve Goldberg will be an enduring blessing!

CPSIA information can be obtained
at www.ICGtesting.com
Printed in the USA
FFHW010655120419
51686142-57117FF

9 781946 124548